Coffee

Jonathan Morris is Research Professor at the University of Hertfordshire. He is a historian of consumption and consumer societies, co-editor of *Coffee: The Comprehensive Guide to the Bean, the Beverage and the Industry* (2013), and a judge for the Specialty Coffee Association's Best Product in Show awards.

Edible

Series Editor: Andrew F. Smith

Edible is a revolutionary series of books dedicated to food and drink that explores the rich history of cuisine. Each book reveals the global history and culture of one type of food or beverage.

Other Titles in the Series

Rice: A Global History by Renee Marton

Saffron: A Global History by Ramin Ganeshram

Chocolate: A Global History by Sarah Moss and Alexander Badenoch

Cocktails: A Global History by Joseph M. Carlin

Tea: A Global History by Helen Saberi

Forthcoming in the Series

Honey: A Global History by Lucy M. Long

Mustard: A Global History by Demet Güzey

Mango: A Global History by Constance L. Kirker and Mary Newman

Ice Cream: A Global History by Laura B. Weiss

Cheese: A Global History by Andrew Dalby

Coffee

A Global History

JONATHAN MORRIS

MACMILLAN

My parents, Anne and Graham Morris, taught me little about coffee, but much about life, and this book is dedicated to them with love.

First published in the United Kingdom 2019 by Reaktion Books Ltd
First published in India 2025 by Macmillan
an imprint of Pan Macmillan Publishing India Private Limited
707 Kailash Building
26 K. G. Marg, New Delhi 110001
www.panmacmillan.co.in

Pan Macmillan, The Smithson, 6 Briset St, Farringdon, London EC1M 5NR
Associated companies throughout the world
www.panmacmillan.com

ISBN 978-93-6113-762-4

1 3 5 7 9 8 6 4 2

Printed and bound in India by Thomson Press India Ltd.

Contents

Introduction

Coffee is a global beverage. It is grown commercially on four continents, and consumed enthusiastically in all seven: Antarctic scientists love their coffee. There is even an Italian espresso machine on the International Space Station. Coffee's journey has taken it from the forests of Ethiopia to the *fincas* of Latin America, from Ottoman coffee houses to 'third wave' cafés, and from the coffee pot to the capsule machine.

This book is the first global history of coffee written by a professional historian. It explains how the world acquired a taste for coffee, yet why coffee tastes so different throughout the world. From the beverage's first appearance among Sufi sects in fifteenth-century Arabia, through to the specialty coffee consumers of twenty-first-century Asia, this book discusses who drank coffee, why and where they drank it, how they prepared it and what it tasted like. It identifies the regions and ways in which coffee was grown, who worked the farms and who owned them, and how the beans were processed, traded and transported. It analyses the businesses behind coffee – the brokers, roasters and machine manufacturers – and dissects the geopolitics behind the structures linking producers to consumers.

Regional Distribution of Global Coffee Production (%)[1]

	Africa and Arabia	Caribbean	Asia	Latin America
1700	100	0	0	0
1830	2	38	28	32
1900–1904	1	4	4	91
1970–74	30	3	6	61
2011–15	9	1	32	58

The distinctions between commodity and specialty coffee, and the ways these determine the transformations that coffee undergoes from seed to cup, are the subject of the opening chapter of the book.

The history of coffee is divided into five eras. Coffee first served as the 'Wine of Islam', cultivated on Yemen's mountain terraces and traded among the Muslim peoples around the shores of the Indian Ocean and the Red Sea. Europeans turned it into a colonial good during the eighteenth century, compelling serfs and slaves to plant it in places as far apart as Java and Jamaica.

Coffee was transformed into an industrial product in the second half of the nineteenth century as the rapid expansion of output in Brazil nurtured the development of a mass consumer market in the United States. After the 1950s, coffee became a global commodity as Africa and Asia regained a significant share of world trade by planting Robusta, a hardier, but harsher-tasting species, used in cheaper blends and soluble products. A movement to recast coffee as a 'specialty beverage' began as a reaction against commodification at the end of the twentieth century. Its transnational success may result in the fifth era of coffee history.

Steampunk coffee machine. This unique machine was built from a variety of upcycled components to create a talking piece for the 2017 London Coffee Festival. At its heart is a cold drip coffee maker that takes eight hours to produce 1 litre of coffee.

The coffee trade operates with a multitude of definitions and units of measurement. Historical data sets are rarely comparable, so rather than imposing a false unity, the book presents statistics in the form they were originally produced. Macro comparisons, calculated using multiple sources, are intended to convey the direction and scale of change, and numbers should not be regarded as definitive.

Grab a cup, turn the page, and enjoy your journey through coffee's global history.

anatomy

THE CO

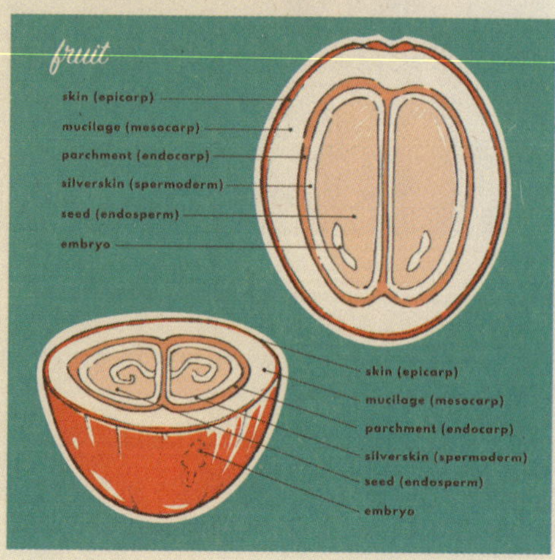

Coff

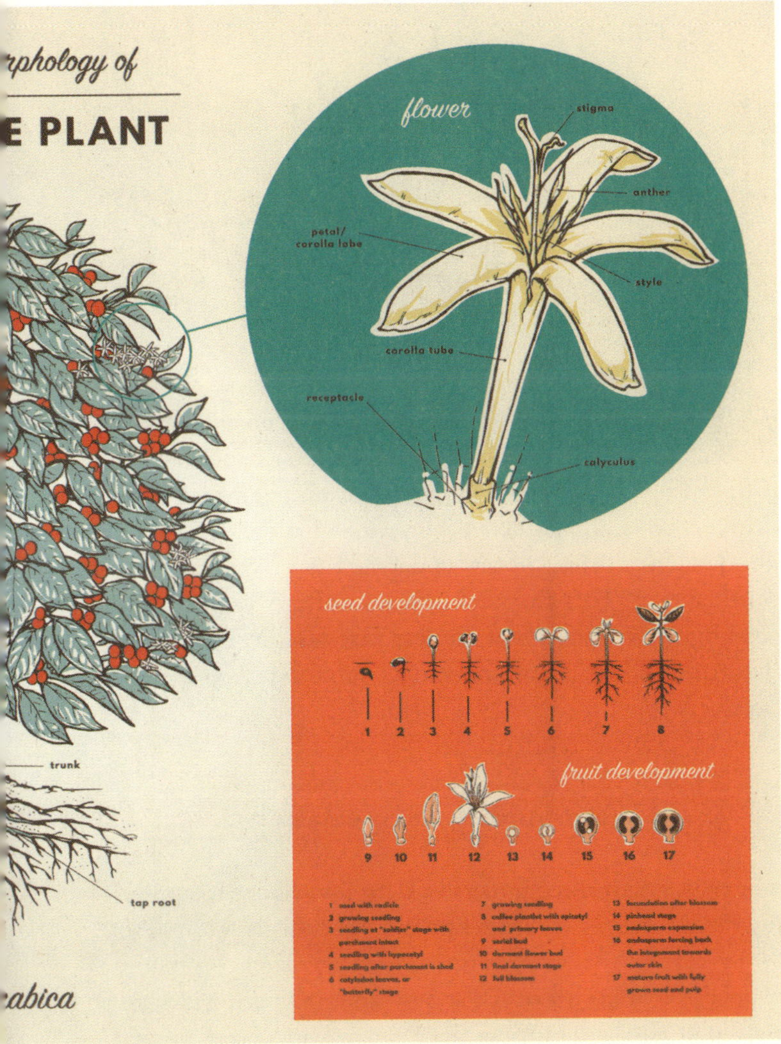

The anatomy and morphology of the coffee plant.

I
Seed to Cup

Coffee is an everyday drink – whether gulped down first thing at breakfast, during a mid-morning break, as an afternoon pick-me-up or as a digestion aid after dinner. Most coffee drinkers have an instinctive sense of what they consider a good cup of coffee, yet few understand what contributes to producing it. This chapter explores coffee's journey from seed to cup. It shows how choices made during this journey determine if the beans are sold as commodity or specialty products.

Commodity or Specialty?

The major reason consumers lack the knowledge to appreciate their coffee is that the industry obscures its complexity and diversity by turning it into a homogenized commodity. Batches of beans harvested at one time are mixed with those picked at another; outputs from farms with different characteristics are combined; sacks from different regions are exported under the same label; green coffees are bought through an exchange where they are never actually seen, before the beans are roasted and blended with others from different countries to be sold under a brand label communicating generic characteristics: 'Rich', 'Mellow' or 'Roaster's Choice'.

Such strategies allow coffee from one source to be substituted with another. Natural events like drought, frost or disease, or man-made ones such as war, can set back coffee production in a region for years. Farmers, exporters, brokers and roasters use homogenization as a risk-management strategy. At least 90 per cent of world coffee production enters the commodity sector.

The remaining 5–10 per cent is 'specialty coffee': high-quality coffee with a distinctive flavour profile and identifiable geographical origins. Like wine, a coffee's flavour is reflective of the variety grown, the district's micro-environment (*terroir*), the growing season's prevalent climatic conditions, and the care with which it is harvested, processed, stored and shipped. Wine contains around three hundred compounds affecting its flavour; for coffee the figure is estimated to be well over a thousand. This 'special(i)ty' sector (Europeans used to include the 'i', Americans don't) has grown exponentially over the last thirty years.

Coffee farms can be divided into three types. Large agribusinesses located on huge Brazilian estates constitute less than 1 per cent of all farms, but produce roughly 10 per cent of the world's supply. Family-owned enterprises, commonly found in Central America and Colombia, make up 5 per cent of farms but account for 30 per cent of output, much of specialty quality. Smallholdings of fewer than 5 hectares (12 acres) number 95 per cent of all coffee farms and produce 60 per cent of global output. On most of these farms coffee is grown as a cash crop within a subsistence regime.[1]

Arabica

Coffee is a gift from Africa, where over 130 species of the genus *Coffea* have been identified. The Arabica coffee plant, *Coffea arabica*, evolved in the southwestern Ethiopian highlands and bordering regions of Kenya and South Sudan, where it still grows wild today. Today Arabica is grown commercially throughout the tropics. It cannot survive outside this belt as the plants die if the temperature falls below freezing. Arabica was the first – and until the twentieth century, the only – species of coffee grown for human consumption. Currently it accounts for around two-thirds of world production.

The Arabica coffee plant is a woody perennial evergreen shrub that, in the wild, grows 9–12 metres (30–40 ft) high under the forest's semi-shade canopy. It is commonly inaccurately referred to as a tree. It is self-pollinating, producing a cluster of small, white, fragrant flowers. The number and size of flowers is largely weather dependent. Showers spark the plant's blossom, but the fruits set best in dry conditions. In

Arabica coffee plants, such as this one in India, produce flowers and fruits along the length of their lateral spurs. Coffee can crop twice in a year with blossoms and cherries present together on the tree.

Stages in the ripening of the coffee cherry. The fruits should be picked when deep red, discarding overripe cherries such as that on the far right.

Ethiopian forest coffee. These semi-wild Arabica coffee plants growing under the forest canopy are tended by smallholders. The beans are described as 'heirloom coffee', the result of centuries of interbreeding between different subspecies in the wild.

semi-dry climates, there is one flowering season; where rainfall is greater there may be two or more, with fruit and flowers simultaneously on the plant. The seeds at the flower's base develop into drupes, referred to as coffee cherries. These ripen 30–35 weeks after flowering, changing colour from green to deep red (yellow in some varieties), at which point they are ready to harvest.

Each cherry contains two flat-faced seeds, commonly, if inaccurately, referred to as beans. Each seed is covered by a parchment layer, and protected by sweet, soft, pinkish pulp under the skin. Occasionally a single rounded seed develops. This is known as a peaberry. Producers separate these from the rest of the crop to be sold at a premium, arguing that they offer better sensory qualities and that the shape is conducive to even roasting. Sceptics suggest the higher price compensates for the fact that a peaberry weighs less than two ordinary beans.

Robusta

During the last three decades of the nineteenth century, the coffee world was transformed by a devastating outbreak of leaf rust that virtually wiped out production in Asia. Coffee cultivators, notably in the Dutch East Indies, started searching for alternative species. They tried *Coffea liberica*, or Liberian coffee, but this too proved susceptible to rust. They then shifted to *Coffea canephora*, known as Robusta, which was sourced from the Congo, via Belgium.

Robusta is not only rust resistant, but it tolerates higher temperatures and humidity than Arabica, making it capable of flourishing at lower elevations. The tree has an umbrella shape, with smaller but more numerous cherries gathered in clusters, making it easier to harvest. Its easy cultivation enabled it to be used as an entrée into coffee production, most recently by Vietnam. Currently Robusta forms around 35–40 per cent of world output.

Robusta suffers from one major defect: it produces poorer-quality coffee than Arabica. A common Robusta tasting note descriptor is burnt rubber. It is nearly always used as part of

Robusta coffee cherries, such as these in Indonesia, are smaller and rounder than Arabica, and develop in large centralized clusters.

a blend, and is often used in instant or soluble coffee products. Coffees marketed as specialty Robustas (notably from India) are usually the result of better husbandry and processing practices. Robusta also contains twice the caffeine levels of Arabica.

Varieties

For most of coffee history, only two varieties of Arabica were cultivated. The commercial variety closest to wild Ethiopian coffee is known as Typica. Bourbon, a natural mutation that occurred in the colony where the French first planted coffee, is the other. Bourbon is higher yielding and tends to produce fruit flavours in contrast to Typica's floral ones.

Brazilian coffee researchers developed the dwarf cultivars Caturra and Catuai, which became popular in the post-war era because of their high yields and easier cultivation. Caturra was interbred with a naturally occurring Arabica-Robusta hybrid,

Timor, to produce Catimor, another high-yielding dwarf with greater disease resistance that could be planted at lower elevations. These were popular among commodity farmers but coffee aficionados were sceptical about their quality in the cup.

During the twenty-first century, however, the specialty world has shown much greater interest in varieties. Geisha (or Gesha), a natural Ethiopian variety, is primarily responsible for this. It was introduced into Central America in the 1950s but gained few followers due to its low yields. In 2004, however, the Peterson family, new owners of the La Esmerelda estate in Boquete, Panama, identified these beans as the source of their farm's individual cup flavour. They separated them out and entered them into the Specialty Coffee Association of America's Roaster's Guild cupping competition, winning three years in a row. In 2007 one lot sold for over one hundred times the price of commodity coffee.

Unsurprisingly Geisha, which produces a cup of complex aromatic and floral flavours with a body like tea, is now being grown on many farms, while other varieties such as Pacamara and Yellow Bourbon have become sought after. In 2018 a natural processed Geisha from Panama was auctioned for a new world record price of $803/lb, when the commodity coffee price was $1.11/lb.[2]

Terroir

The micro-environment, or *terroir*, where a coffee crop is cultivated has a substantial effect on its flavour profile. Discerning a direct line between any one single factor and outcomes in the cup is hazardous, due to the difficulty of isolating the multiple variables involved.

Coffee grows best at high altitudes on nutrient-rich, frequently volcanic, soils, such as here in El Salvador.

The most important elements are temperature and elevation. Arabica becomes unproductive at temperatures over 32°C, so elevation is essential to avoid these. In the equatorial zone within 10 degrees latitude of the Equator, suitable conditions are usually found above 900 metres (2,950 ft); at the subtropical extremes, elevations can be much lower. The best Ethiopian coffees, such as those from the Yirgacheffe district, are grown at around 1,800 metres (5,905 ft), whereas Hawaii's celebrated Kona coffee belt starts 200 metres (656 ft) above sea level.

Within a region, the higher the altitude at which coffee is grown, the better the bean quality. Higher-grown coffees possess more concentrated flavours, possibly due to the greater difference between day- and night-time temperatures. Beans grown at lower levels are softer, less dense and age more rapidly. El Salvador grades its coffee by elevation; the top-grade 'Strictly High Grown' is grown above 1,200 metres (3,937 ft).

The average air temperature has a significant effect on the sensory profile of the bean, with cooler temperatures being correlated with positive features such as acidity (experienced on the palette as liveliness) and fruit flavours, whereas high temperatures can result in reduced aromatic quality and an increase in off-flavours. Surveys of the main Arabica-producing areas suggest that the ideal conditions for producing specialty coffee are found in zones where the temperature is relatively constant throughout the year, ranging from 13°C in the coolest month to 25°C in the hottest. These conditions obtain only in a quarter of the land used for Arabica cultivation.[3]

Coffee can be grown in a wide variety of soil types, providing they are deep, well drained and rich in nutrients. Volcanic soils are particularly favoured and some believe these correlate with greater acidity. Similarly, coffee flourishes in a wide variety of climate regimes, providing it receives the equivalent of 125 centimetres (49 in.) of rainfall a year. This can be distributed either evenly or seasonally, or delivered artificially via irrigation systems.

Coffee grows naturally in partial shade, requiring only 25 per cent sunlight to develop efficiently. The impact of shade on taste profiles is contentious. Research in Costa Rica suggested shade promoted better acidity, less bitterness and lower astringency, yet a study in Colombia suggested the reverse, while one in Hawaii found no difference in cup quality between shade and sun-grown coffee of the same type.[4]

Cultivation

Farmers cultivate coffee from seed, and transplant potted plants into fields at around eighteen months. Saplings usually begin fruiting at three to four years of age and reach commercial maturity at around five to seven years. The trees develop vertical shoots from which lateral spurs grow outwards. Fruit

A coffee seedling nursery on a large coffee estate in Brazil.

sets in clusters along the previous year's laterals. Pruning restricts the trees' height to 8–10 metres (26–33 ft) to facilitate picking.

There is no theoretical limit to the productive life of a tree providing it remains healthy. However, when stressed (by lack of food or water), the coffee plant will literally sacrifice itself to preserve that year's crop, letting its leaves yellow and its branches die back to the point of no recovery.

Shade alleviates stress, moderating air and soil temperature extremes and reducing the plants' need for food. In the absence of natural shade, trees can be planted to serve as windbreaks and stabilize slopes, preventing soil erosion. Peasant farmers frequently shade their coffee plants with subsistence crops.

Growers wanting high yields often adopt dense planting schemes where coffee trees self-shade each other, creating 'coffee hedges'. This drives down individual plant yield, but significantly increases the overall yield per hectare. This approach lends itself to mechanized farming and is commonly found on large Brazilian commercial coffee plantations. Such 'sun-grown' or 'technified' coffee requires greater amounts of fertilizers and frequent weeding and is more susceptible to disease, not least due to the reduction in birdlife preying on insects.

Coffee leaf rust caused by the fungus *Hemileia vastatrix* is the most damaging disease prevalent in coffee. Orange and yellow spots appear on the leaves which then drop off. Defoliation kills branches and eventually the plant itself. An outbreak in the Central Americas in 2011 affected 70 per cent of farms over five years, causing 1.7 million coffee workers to lose their jobs.[5] The coffee berry borer, a small black beetle that lays its eggs at the coffee cherry's centre, is the chief insect threat. Once the larvae hatch they eat their way out of the bean. An acute infestation can destroy around 50 per cent of the crop.

Harvesting

While *terroir* and variety are responsible for the coffee's flavour profile, it is primarily harvesting and processing practices that determine the quality of the lot produced.

The coffee cherries are either picked or stripped from the tree. A high-quality coffee can only be produced from a consistent batch of fully ripened beans, so pickers select individual cherries, leaving others on the branch to reach maturity. Selective picking is labour and cost intensive. It requires small producers to band together, helping harvest each other's crops, while larger estates recruit seasonal workers, and incentivize them to exercise quality control while picking.

Stripping, by contrast, involves removing all the berries from the branch by grasping it with one hand while running the other hand down its length. The cherries (and other debris) land on the ground, or in pre-positioned nets, and are then

Selective hand-picking in Hawaii. These plants are of the Typica variety of Arabica coffee.

sorted for processing. Commodity market producers generally use the stripping method, taking advantage of the relative predictability of rainy (hence flowering) periods, to estimate when around 75 per cent of the crop will have matured.

On flatland plantations, harvesting machines perform a mechanical form of stripping, passing along the coffee hedges. It has been calculated that five workers using machinery on a Brazilian plantation can harvest the same amount of coffee in three days as a thousand pickers working for one day in the mountainous regions of Guatemala.[6]

Natural Processing

Processing removes the cherry's protective layers surrounding the bean. First the skin and pulp surrounding the stone are removed using either a 'dry' or 'wet' processing method. The coffee is then sent for milling to remove the remaining parchment left covering the bean.

Section through a coffee cherry. Each seed is surrounded by a sticky mucilage and protected by the soft pink pulp between it and the skin.

The first stage of natural processing: cherries being dried on a patio in Brazil.

Naturally dried coffee cherries prior to hulling, Brazil.

Natural, or 'dry', processing involves spreading the coffee cherries out on a concrete patio in the sun, and periodically turning them as the fruit dries out and decomposes. Using rakes, the coffee is shaped into rows of about 5 centimetres (2 in.) in height, with patches of bare patio between them. The coffee is periodically shifted into the bare space, leaving the space previously occupied by the coffee to dry. The whole process takes around two weeks, after which the beans are ready for hulling.

Natural processing is particularly suited to environments where water is in short supply. In the Yemen, where the technique first developed, coffee can be seen drying on the flat roofs of the houses in mountain villages where it is grown. The process accentuates the body and fruitiness of the coffee, as well as creating a 'wild' tang in the aftertaste. Done well, the flavours can be exhilarating; done badly, they can recall a farmyard.

The main attraction of natural processing is its cost-effectiveness. Most commodity coffee is dry-processed: both Brazilian 'natural' Arabica, and nearly all the world's Robusta.

From the quality perspective, the difficulty with the dry process is lack of consistency. The harvested cherries are usually only sorted manually beforehand, increasing the danger that bad cherries will get through and contaminate the rest of the batch. The process is also uneven, with fruits experiencing a variety of temperatures, and there are dangers of excessive fermentation or mould.

Washed

Wet processing tends to produce a smoother coffee with more consistent taste and better acidity. The process begins with the cherries being placed in a flotation tank. The dense ripe cherries sink to the trough's bottom, while both overripe and underdeveloped cherries float on top, along with any detritus like sticks and leaves. These 'floaters' are removed and a pumping system conveys the submerged cherries into a mechanical de-pulper. Here they are broken against a screen,

Underdeveloped and overripe coffee cherries on the top of a flotation tank in Hawaii – the preparatory stage of wet processing.

Drying wet-processed coffee on so-called African tables, Ethiopia.

which prevents the skin and pith passing through with the bean. Underripe cherries are too tough to be broken by the screen, and are removed at this point.

Beans are sent to tanks of clean water where they sit for twelve to fourteen hours while the bean's sticky mucilage is broken down by fermentation. Assessment is often carried out by feeling a handful of beans: when the mucilage has disappeared, the beans are removed.

Wet processing can involve considerable amounts of water, and in recent years both de-pulping and de-mucilator machines have been developed to reduce this. De-mucilator machines sit directly behind the de-pulping screen, rubbing the beans against each other to remove the mucilage, avoiding the need for fermentation.

Once the mucilage is removed, the beans are rinsed in water and then dried down to 11 per cent moisture content. This will be done on either patios or tables, sometimes situated in clear plastic tunnels to harness the greenhouse effect while protecting the coffee. Mechanical dryers are used where the climate dictates.

Pulped Natural and Honey Coffee

The pulped natural method developed in Brazil in the 1980s. In this process the beans were passed through the de-pulper, but then sent directly to the drying patio with their mucilage still attached. It resulted in some outstanding coffees, combining the body obtained from dry processing with the acidity characteristic of wet. Central American producers adopted and modified the process to create honey coffees, which are dried slowly in a more humid environment, developing their aromatic qualities. These are divided into yellow, red and black categories, depending on the amount of mucilage left on the bean – the black retaining all its mucilage and taking up to thirty days to dry.

Animal Processing

Indonesian coffee known as Kopi Luwak is famously processed by palm civet cats. They eat cherries that have fallen to the ground and then excrete beans, effectively performing the de-pulping process. These are collected, washed and finished in the usual way. The enzymes in the cat's digestive system supposedly impart a unique flavour, enabling the coffee to be retailed for upwards of $100/lb, while a single cup of Kopi Luwak in New York can cost $30. Unsurprisingly other countries have now discovered animals capable of performing the same function, including a Vietnamese weasel, Thai elephants and the Brazilian Jacu bird.

Sadly, the fad for Kopi Luwak has resulted in many of the animals being captured and caged to be force-fed coffee beans. Wild certifications do exist but a large proportion of what is sold is presented under false pretences, sometimes

Palm civet cats in front of a market stall that sells Kopi Luwak in Bali.

having been chemically treated. The bottom line with animal-processed coffee is that what comes out reflects what goes in, and producers can cut costs by using cheaper cherries. The usual qualities ascribed to Kopi Luwak are low acidity and lack of bitterness – these are more about moderating bad coffee than enhancing the good stuff.

Resting

After the beans have been processed and dried, they will ideally be left to 'rest' in their parchment, stored away from the elements, for one to two months prior to milling. This allows them to mature, losing the grassy taste of freshly processed coffee.

In India's southwestern Malabar region, resting coffee is stored in open warehouses exposed to monsoon winds and humidity. This results in the beans changing colour to a golden yellow and swelling up as their moisture content rises

Dried coffee left in its parchment to rest prior to milling.

to 13–14 per cent. The results mimic the effects of the long sea journeys undertaken by coffee during the nineteenth century, and produce a mellow coffee low in acidity.

Milling

After resting, the remaining parchment is removed from the bean by a hulling machine. The coffee is then graded by size, using a tilted sorting table. Standard sizes are measured in diameters of 64ths of an inch (usually 10–20). Kenyan AA is size 18, for example. Defective beans are also removed during milling, either by hand or using a colour-sorting machine to identify unripe, broken or insect-damaged beans.

After milling is completed, the green coffee is packed into burlap or hessian sacks made from jute. These protect the coffee from sun and rain, while allowing air to flow through the beans, thus avoiding mildew. The air circulation can give rise to staling, and petroleum-based coatings can leave a

A mechanical grading table in operation. The table tilts and vibrates as the beans travel along it, so they are sorted by density.

so-called 'baggy' taste. In recent years, specialty producers have started placing green coffee into large multilayered plastic bags that create a gas- and moisture-proof barrier before sealing them into the sacks. The standard sack size is 60 kilograms (132 lb). Many trade statistics are quantified in sacks, rather than by weight.

Classification

By the time the bags arrive at the shipping port, the coffee will have changed hands several times. Washing stations and milling plants require capital investment and production volumes that small farmers cannot afford. In some origins, nearly all the supply chain links are in private hands, with growers selling their beans to middlemen at the farm gate; in others, farmers operate cooperative washing stations, and sell their coffee collectively to mills. Export agencies are the last recipients of the processed coffee in the country of origin, preparing and packing it to be shipped to overseas consumer markets.

At each stage along the supply chain, individual lots become mixed into bigger batches based on the standardized categories utilized by the producer country. Brazil, for example, recognizes seven coffee grades defined principally in relation to the number of permitted defects within a sample: these include the number of overripe, broken or diseased beans, as well as stones, husks, twigs and so on. These broad classifications can be related to the prevailing prices operating in world markets, thus allowing coffee to be traded as a commodity.

International Trading

This is done through the two leading coffee futures trading markets: the New York International Commodity Exchange (ICE) for Arabica and the London International Financial Futures and Options Exchange (LIFFE) for Robusta. In both, a standard contract is traded for the delivery of mainstream coffee at a predetermined future date. In New York the traded contract is the 'C' contract: a consignment delivery of 37,500 lbs (or 17,000 kg) of washed mild Arabica coffee with a rating of 9–23 defects within a 12 oz (or 350 g) sample. Lots with fewer defects are traded at a premium, while below-par lots are sold at a discount. The 'C' contract covers coffee from twenty producer countries, with some, such as Colombia, enjoying automatic premiums, while others, including the Dominican Republic, are discounted. Ten delivery months are quoted over a two-year period, with a trading position closed a month before delivery.

These futures exchanges are important for the coffee-trading industry. As the exchange logs all contracts agreed between brokers for future coffee deliveries, an indicator price emerges. Some, though few, of these contracts result in physical coffee deliveries as per the exchange's rules and standard contracts. A greater volume of physical coffee is traded via forward contracts, incorporating the standard futures price as a base point from which the final price for a particular grade of coffee is calculated. So a tender including a differential might be quoted for delivery of grade *x* from country *y* for shipment in October at New York December +10 (that is, the price for the December delivered 'C' contract' plus 10 points).

This leaves uncertainty over the final price, which can be offset or hedged by using the exchange's futures and options markets. Trading in options (the option, not the obligation, to make or take delivery of a futures contract at a certain price threshold or expiration period) began in 1986 in New York. It has brought many speculators into the market, to the point that in 2015 the volume of contracts traded was 27 times that

Brokers trading Robusta futures contracts on the London International Financial Futures and Options Exchange (LIFFE). London, 1980s.

of world Arabica production.[7] This gap between the physical and traded volumes of green coffee is beneficial to traders, as the liquidity generated means it is easier for brokers to hedge their positions. They transfer price fluctuation risks from themselves to financial speculators. Conversely, increasing speculation results in greater price volatility, which impacts others in the value chain, such as growers and small roasters, who do not have access to the futures market.

Shipping

Brokers acquire control of green coffee by buying in spot markets at either exporting or importing ports. The commodity coffee market is dominated by a few leading brokerage networks. The largest is the Hamburg-based Neumann Kaffee Group, which handles 10 per cent of world coffee demand. Brokerages manage coffee movement logistics, such as warehousing and shipping, and delivering to roasters who have usually purchased via contract options. Coffee is shipped in containers, each one holding around 275 bags of coffee. Entire shipments destined for one roaster may be loaded into a single container, with the beans air blown into it and sucked out into silos at the journey's end.

The major U.S. receiving ports are New York and New Orleans. (The latter's closure in 2005 due to Hurricane Katrina provoked a brief scare that America would run out of coffee.) In Europe, the leading centre is Antwerp, which warehouses roughly half the coffee arriving into the Continent.

Decaffeination

Decaffeination plants are usually located in port hinterlands. Green beans are steamed then soaked in hot water, inducing them to swell up. This enables the solvents used – methylene chloride or ethyl acetate – to remove the caffeine from the beans. The solvent is drained, the caffeine extract sold off and the beans steam cleaned and dried. Liquid or supercritical carbon dioxide can also be used under very high pressures. This is costly but removes fewer additional compounds. Alternatively, using a process developed in Switzerland, hot water can be used as the solvent. After eight hours or so, the beans are drained, and the water is passed through charcoal filter beds to remove the caffeine. The water is then concentrated, and returned to the beans so they can reabsorb the

Samples of caffeinated and decaffeinated green coffee.

remaining flavours. The process is performed using batches of beans with the water from one lot being returned to a subsequent one.

Roasting

The retail coffee-roasting business is dominated by large, multinational food conglomerates such as Nestlé, Jacobs Douwe Egberts, J. M. Smucker (owners of Folgers), Kraft Heinz (Maxwell House) and Tchibo. Medium-sized roasters frequently produce their own brand labelled coffee for supermarket retailers and grocery chains, and supply the HORECA (hotel, restaurant and catering) trade. Niche roasters often concentrate on specialty coffees, including single origins and estates, while micro roasters produce small batches of coffee primarily for sale in their own shops and local supply networks.

The basic principle of coffee roasting is that beans are heated evenly to a final temperature of between 200°C and 250°C. Most roasters use a so-called drum roaster in which the beans are rotated in a metal cylinder situated above a flame. These machines usually roast one batch at a time, with each batch lasting between eight and twenty minutes, depending on the finish required. Large industrial producers may use continuously operating fluid bed roasters in which the beans are blasted with pressurized jets of hot air for around two minutes.

During roasting the green beans turn yellow, then light brown as they lose their moisture and the starches are caramelized and converted to sugars. A 'first crack' is heard at around 205°C as the beans break open under pressure from the gases building up inside them. The beans continue to brown until a second crack occurs at around 225°C as the cell walls collapse

The freshly roasted coffee in this drum roaster has just been discharged into the cooling tray.

and glossy oils are exuded onto the bean's surface. If roasting is continued, the remaining sugars will carbonize, and the coffee turns black.

The two main factors in determining the coffee's flavour are the degree of roast and the speed of roasting. Artisan roasters will adjust their machines according to their interpretations of the sounds and smells emanating from their machine, as well as the appearance of beans extracted using a sampler. Many machines can be programmed to perform a particular roast to order.

Lighter roasts, developed slowly to a point somewhere between the first and second crack, are believed to bring out the best in most specialty coffees. Aromas, flavours and acidity will decrease with further roasting, whereas body and bitterness increase. Sweetness peaks somewhere between the first and second crack as the sugars caramelize before starting to turn bitter. After the second crack, the flavours from the roast overpower those from the beans, which is why dark roasts are often used for lesser-quality coffees such as Robusta.

Once the roast is completed, the beans must be cooled as quickly as possible to prevent further cooking: most drum roasting machines deposit them into a perforated tray where they are stirred while cool air is drawn through them. Alternatively, the beans may be sprayed or dipped in water. As the beans absorb water, commodity roasters will often use cooling as a pretext for increasing the weight (and hence value) of the coffee.

Instant

Instant or soluble coffee is produced by freeze-drying or spray drying. An extract is prepared from roast and ground coffee with pressurised water at 175°C, concentrated, and frozen to minus 40°C. It is broken up into small granules, and dried in a heated vacuum chamber. The frozen water within the granules sublimates directly into vapour that is removed by condenser. Spray drying, the older and cheaper process, requires the concentrate to be sprayed into a drying tower, where it turns into a dehydrated powder as it falls through a stream of air heated to 250°C.

Blending

Roasters blend to develop distinctive taste profiles for their brands and to manage costs. Coffee blends are usually based on unwashed Brazilian Arabicas (known as Naturals or Santos) whose relative neutrality means they can form the blend's bulk. Character is then added by incorporating

Colombian or other so-called Milds with more distinctive features. Low-cost, mass-market blends begin with a Robusta base, adding Santos and topping out with coffee from other origins. High-quality blends usually combine the beans after each lot has been roasted to its own sweet point; however, it is more cost-efficient to combine the beans before and roast them together, so mass-market roasters use a one-size-fits-all approach.

The roaster's art lies in adjusting the roasts and blends of the available coffee so that the taste profile for a brand remains consistent even if its contents have changed. Often this involves substituting one coffee type with another: some roasters agree forward contracts with brokers in which the coffee delivered can be varied according to availability. For example, a Robusta contract might allow for either Ugandan standard grade or Ivory Coast grade 2.

Cupping

After roasting, the coffee's flavour notes acquired throughout its cultivation and processing can be appreciated. Roasters check for quality and consistency by 'cupping' the final product. The same procedure is used to evaluate samples from brokers, and by buyers and producers in the origin country. Comparative cupping uses identically sized parcels of green coffees in a sample roaster so each is prepared similarly. The beans are ground and placed into porcelain cups. Cuppers evaluate the aroma of the dry samples, after which hot water is added. The cuppers then check the wet aroma. After a four-minute wait, they use a spoon to 'break' the surface's crust, putting their noses as close as possible to the cup to catch the aroma, and then slurp spoonfuls of coffee with as much air as possible to spray the coffee around the tongue's taste buds.

The Coffee Quality Institute's Q cupping scheme has been adopted by the specialty coffee world as a method of standardizing cuppers' assessments. All certified Q graders are trained and examined to ensure consistency. Scores are allotted for fragrance/aroma (dry and wet), acidity, flavour, body, aftertaste, uniformity, clean cup, balance, sweetness and overall impression, after which deductions are made for defects to give an overall score out of 100. Coffees scoring over 80 are considered specialty standard.

Packaging

Before it leaves the roastery, the coffee will be allowed to de-gas (expelling the carbon dioxide build-up from roasting) for up to three days before being packaged into airtight or vacuum packs. Most coffee is now pre-ground at the factory for consumer convenience, although this accelerates staling once the pack is opened, because a greater proportion of the coffee's surface area is exposed to oxygen. Higher-grade coffee is often sealed into bags with a one-way valve, allowing the beans to continue expelling gas without air entering, while some coffees are nitrogen-flushed to remove oxygen from the package entirely.

Brewing

There are innumerable procedures and equipment for brewing coffee. They can be divided into four basic methods:

Coffee brewing equipment. From left to right: AeroPress, french press/ cafetière, V60 hand filter, Chemex and a syphon brewer.

1. Boiling – ground coffee and water are heated together, as with Turkish coffee;
2. Immersion – hot water is added to the coffee, as with French press;
3. Percolation – hot water is passed through the grounds, as with filter;
4. Pressure brewing – hot water is passed with pressure through the grounds, speeding up extraction rates, as with espresso.

An industry saying is that it takes a year for coffee to travel from field to cup, and a minute for the consumer to mess it up. To avoid doing so, see the Recipes section in this book.

Health

The brewing method chosen is one determinant of the caffeine level of the final beverage. The longer water is in contact with the coffee, the more caffeine it absorbs. Other key determinants are beverage size and, most importantly, the proportion of Robusta in the blend, as this contains twice the caffeine of Arabica. The U.S. government's *Dietary Guidelines for Americans, 2015–2020* suggest that a standard 8 fl. oz (235 ml) serving of drip-brewed coffee would contain 96 mg of caffeine, a similar sized cup of instant 66 mg, and a 1 fl. oz (30 ml) single espresso 64 mg. Such average figures vary wildly, but it is worth noting that the guidelines also state that consumption of up to 400 mg a day can be regarded as healthy.[8]

Caffeine is a stimulant that can increase brain function and combat drowsiness. Brain activity is normally regulated by adenosine, which binds to receptors on the surfaces of nerve cells, inducing sleep and causing the blood vessels to dilate to receive more oxygen. When caffeine crosses from the bloodstream into the brain, it binds to the nerve cells' receptors, preventing the adenosine from reaching them, while the blood vessels contract, reducing headaches. Adrenaline production is increased, raising alertness, and dopamine reabsorption is slowed down, heightening a sense of pleasure. Therefore, coffee drinkers can use the beverage to 'kick start' the morning, keep them awake on the night shift, relieve stress headaches or simply to feel good.

Consuming too much caffeine over a short period can be detrimental to health. It can increase heart rate and blood pressure, provoking a caffeine-induced version of 'the jitters', accompanied by symptoms like light-headedness, anxiety, insomnia and diarrhoea. The question is, how much is *too* much? Caffeine concentration in the brain reaches its maximum around one hour after drinking coffee, while its usual half-life in the body is three to four hours. Caffeine metabolization varies between individuals, with factors such as weight, genetics, gender and lifestyle contributing significantly. Overconsumption of caffeine can build dependency (hence withdrawal headaches for 'java junkies'), but it can also build tolerance to its effects.

The combination of caffeine's variation in a single serving of coffee and the range of individual responses to the drug explain why it is almost impossible to produce any meaningful recommendations about suitable levels of coffee consumption. Public health surveys are bedevilled by reporting problems. One person's cup of coffee will be a different size, blend and brewing process to another's, even before accounting for any impact of milk and sugar.

Current studies are discovering many positive associations with coffee consumption, suggesting that coffee's chemicals have a role in protecting against liver disease, kidney, bowel and, to a lesser extent, breast cancer, and that coffee may decrease the risk of Alzheimer's and Parkinson's diseases because of its high levels of antioxidants. Coffee has been cleared of having a dehydrating or diuretic effect and may assist in combating adult-onset diabetes. Recent studies suggest that coffee drinkers live longer. According to the editor of the *American Journal of Medicine*, coffee lovers should 'partake and enjoy this mild and perhaps beneficial addiction'.[9]

A Bedouin in early 20th-century Transjordania roasts beans in a portable pan over the fire. The flat, bulbous bottom sections of the Arabian coffee pots known as *dallahs* enable them to stand upright in the sand.

2
Wine of Islam

Coffee has a 'foundation myth', much beloved by marketers, that one day Kaldi, a young Ethiopian goatherd, noticed his animals became agitated after eating a shrub's red berries. Kaldi chewed the berries himself and ended up 'dancing' around. Kaldi was then either discovered by, or went to consult with, an imam, who also sampled the berries. He either a) found they kept him awake during late-night prayers so turned them into an infusion to share with others; or b) threw them in the fire in disgust only to smell their delicious aroma, deciding to retrieve them from the embers, grind them up, add hot water and drink the resulting beverage!

The Kaldi story first appeared in Europe in 1671 as part of a coffee treatise published by Antonio Fausto Naironi, a Maronite Christian from the Levant (today's Lebanon) who had emigrated to Rome. He likely heard it in his homeland. Exactly when, where and in what forms humans first came to consume coffee cannot be definitively established. There are rumours of charred beans being found at ancient sites, and some suggest herbs and decoctions described in the *Canon of Medicine* by the Persian physician and philosopher Ibn Sīnā (980–1037), also known as Avicenna, derive from the coffee plant.

It is certain that for the first two hundred or so years of coffee's recorded existence, between 1450 and 1650, it was consumed almost exclusively by Muslim peoples whose custom sustained a coffee economy centred around the Red Sea. This was the world from which modern versions of the drink evolved and the foundations of the contemporary coffee house format laid.

The Oromo tribe, occupying a large swathe of southern Ethiopia, including the Kaffa and Buno regions in which Arabica coffee is indigenous, prepare a variety of foodstuffs and beverages utilizing different elements of the plant. These include *kuti*, tea made from lightly roasted young plant leaves, *hoja*, combining the berry's dried skins with cow's milk, and *bunna qela*, in which dried coffee beans are roasted with butter and salt to produce a solid stimulating snack, carried on expeditions and eaten to heighten energy levels.

The story of Kaldi as depicted in the national coffee museum, Ethiopia, 2017. In front of the panel, a hostess is waiting to serve coffee being made in the jebena – the black clay coffee kettle – to her right.

Buna is the most well known. Dried coffee husks are simmered in boiling water for fifteen minutes before the resultant beverage is served. Today, coffee farmers have started selling a similar product named *cascara*, consisting of the dried cherry skins removed during processing, brewed as a fruit tea. Originally the beverage was prepared with the cherry's entire desiccated remains – skin, pulp and stone.

Named *qishr* in Arabic, this infusion appears to have made its way across the 32 kilometres (20 mi.) of the Bab-el-Mandeb straits at the southern end of the Red Sea during the mid-fifteenth century. It was adopted by the Sufi mystic sects in Yemen for use in *dhikrs*: night-time prayers in which the mystics concentrate on God to the exclusion of all else by entering a trance-like state. A stimulating potion called *qahwa*, was incorporated into the ritual's beginning, ladled out by the leader from a large vessel and passed around while the group chanted a mantra, such as, 'There is no God but God, the Master, the Clear Reality.' *Qahwa* was vital because Sufism was practised by laymen who worked during the day: the etymology of the word implies a lessening of desire, presumably for sleep.

Qahwa was originally prepared with *kafta*, the leaves of the *khat* plant. This has hallucinogenic properties that promote a sense of euphoria, but using *qishr* would have assisted in keeping worshippers awake. The switch was supposedly instigated by the Sufi mufti Muhammed al-Dhabani, who died in 1470. He is the first historical personage we can associate with coffee. The Arab scholar Abd al-Qadir al-Jaziri, whose manuscript *Umdat al safwa fi hill al-qahwa*, written around 1556, is the principal information source on coffee's spread in the Islamic world and reproduces an account claiming that al-Dhabani travelled to Ethiopia, notes that

> he found the people using *qahwa* though he knew nothing of its characteristics. After he had returned to Aden, he felt ill, and remembering [*qahwa*], he drank it and benefitted by it. He found that among its properties was that it drove away fatigue and lethargy, and brought to the body a certain sprightliness and vigour. In consequence, when he became a Sufi, he and other Sufis in Aden began to use the beverage made from it.[1]

A second account suggests that although Ali ibn 'Umar al-Shadhili is celebrated as the 'father' of *qahwa* in Mocha, this was made from *khat*, whereas in:

> Aden at the time of . . . al-Dhabani there was no *kafta*, so he said to those that followed him . . . that 'coffee beans . . . promoted wakefulness, so try *qahwa* made from it'. They tried it, and found that it performed the same function . . . with little expense or trouble.[2]

Qahwa initially referred simply to the religious potion, but subsequently became the term for Arabic coffee prepared with beans alone, whereas *qishr* still refers to an infusion of dried fruits and spices.

Sufi practices helped transport coffee knowledge northwards into the Arabian territories, the Hijaz, on the eastern shores of the Red Sea. These included the holy cities of Mecca, Jeddah and Medina. Coffee eventually arrived at Cairo, capital of the ruling Mamluk sultanate, sometime during the 1500s, where it was first used by Yemeni students at the Al-Azhar Islamic university. The driver behind coffee's diffusion in the Near East was its increasing adoption as a social beverage consumed outside religious ceremonies. It was this practice that led to the first, and famous, moment when coffee was effectively 'put on trial' by an Islamic court, in Mecca in 1511.

On patrol one evening, Kh'air Beg, the Mamluk appointed city *pasha* (governor), discovered a group of men drinking *qahwa* in the mosque's grounds. Beg chased the men away and, next morning, convened a meeting of the city's *ulema* (religious scholars) to debate questions surrounding the consumption of coffee. The *ulema* were quick to condemn clandestine meetings but far less convinced that consuming coffee was contrary to Islam.

The argument hinged on whether coffee drinking promoted intoxication, defined as a state in which control over the body is lost. Beg produced three physicians who testified that this was the case, so the *ulema* concurred. Beg used this as a pretext for banning the sale or consumption of coffee, publicly or privately, throughout the city.

Why? Coffee was hardly unknown to Beg – it had been used openly for some time. It was also consumed in establishments, such as wine taverns, that, in theory, only served non-Muslims. It seems likely that Beg's real purpose was to secure greater control over the city. The testifying physicians were well known for their opposition to coffee, perhaps because they feared that its proclaimed benefits would provide competition for their own prescriptions.

Beg's ban did not last long. The judgment was sent to Cairo for ratification. When it was returned, the ban on public gatherings to drink coffee was upheld, but not that on the consumption of coffee itself. In 1512 Beg was dismissed and open consumption on the streets of Mecca returned. It seems likely the Cairo authorities agreed with the judgement of a later writer that it would be impossible to argue that coffee induced intoxication when, 'one drinks coffee with the name of the Lord on his lips, and stays awake, while the person who seeks wanton delight in intoxicants disregards the Lord, and gets drunk.'[3]

Thereafter, coffee continued its diffusion across the Islamic world, assisted by visitors to Mecca who encountered it when making the Hajj pilgrimage. The Ottoman conquest of Egypt in 1516–17 facilitated its spread into the Turkish-run empire, reaching Damascus in 1534 and Istanbul in 1554. Two coffee houses were opened in the capital by Syrians, Hakam and Shem, from Damascus and Aleppo respectively. Situated in the city's downtown quarters, near the port and central markets, these coffee houses attracted an elite clientele, including poets who would try out their latest work on fellow literati, merchants engaged in games such as backgammon and chess, and Ottoman officials conversing with each other while seated upon luxurious couches and carpets. Such was Shems's success, he is said to have returned to Aleppo three years later, having made a profit of 5,000 gold pieces.

There was, however, a notable difference in colour between Arabian coffee and Turkish coffee. Arabic coffee (*qahwa*) was (and is) served as a semi-translucent, light brown liquid. The beans are lightly toasted before being cooled, crushed and mixed with spices such as ginger root, cinnamon and, especially, cardamom. The mixture is placed in a copper-bottomed pot, boiled with water for around fifteen minutes and then decanted into a smaller, pre-heated serving vessel (*dallah*) often with a long spout. The host pours a small cup, or *finjan*, for each guest.

The Ottoman Turks, by contrast, drank a dark, opaque beverage described by a contemporary poet as 'the negro enemy of sleep and love' – the forerunner of Turkish coffee, or *kahve*, today. The beans are blackened by roasting and then ground into a powder. The coffee is placed with water in a *cezve* (known outside Turkey as an *ibrik* or *briki*), a

The traditional Turkish coffee-making apparatus is a *cezve*, a small open pot, equipped with a long handle so it can be placed directly over the fire. The spout enables the coffee to be poured directly into the cups known as *finjans*. Alternatively, for serving, the coffee liquor is transferred into an *ibrik*, such as this Egyptian example, characterized by a long slender spout and high tapered neck. Outside Turkey, variations on the word *ibrik* are used to describe both forms of equipment, as *cezve* was deemed too difficult to pronounce.

wide-bottomed open pot that narrows before reaching a broader rim. It is brought to the boil, removed from the flame and foam from the top of the liquid is spooned into the cups. The liquid may then be brought back to the boil (at least once, often twice), and additional liquor poured into the cups, while an attempt is made to retain the foam structure.

The practice of roasting beans was used by some Istanbul imams to argue that the consumption of coffee was illicit because the carbonization of the beans meant the drink was prepared from an inanimate (therefore forbidden) substance. In 1591 Bostanzade Mehmed Effendi, the Sheik ul-Islam (the highest religious authority), issued a *fatwa*, definitively declaring that the beverage remained of vegetable origin, as complete carbonization had not taken place. According to a contemporary chronicler:

> Among the *ulema*, the sheykhs, the viziers and the great, there was nobody left who did not drink it. It even reached such a point that the grand viziers built great coffee houses as investments, and began to rent them out at one or two gold pieces a day.[4]

The coffee house's appeal lay in providing the first legitimate public space for socialization among Muslim men. At night, convention demanded that decent people should eat at home, so the only places open were those with dubious reputations – the wine taverns and establishments selling *boza*, a mildly alcoholic malt beverage made with fermented cereals. The coffee houses, lit by large, ceiling-suspended lamps, provided a refuge on summer evenings. During Ramadan, many observers chose to break their daytime fasts with a coffee after sunset. Customers could sit outside in shaded and scented gardens, listening to a coffee shop's storyteller or musicians who, at least in the early coffee houses of the Hijaz, might include women songstresses, screened off from the guests' sight.

The advent of the coffee house created possibilities for new forms of social interaction. Previously, entertaining others would have involved inviting them to one's house, providing a banquet, probably prepared by servants, and entailing the display of possessions (and probably wife), all of which created a distinction between host and guest. Now one could meet peers at a coffee house, and exchange hospitality on a more equal footing through the simple expedient of buying each other cups of coffee. The layout of these early coffee

This 1698 print by the Dutch illustrator Jan Luyken illustrates the gender divisions around coffee in the Ottoman Empire. It shows men smoking in a Turkish coffee shop, while a gathering of women enjoy drinking coffee in private. The image was based on travellers' accounts.

houses facilitated an egalitarian ambience, as patrons were seated according to the order in which they arrived, at long benches or on divans running alongside the walls, rather than by their rank.

Alongside the elite, this format enabled those of lesser means to entertain each other and display their generosity. A visitor to Cairo in 1599 noticed:

> When soldiers go . . . into a coffee house and they have to get change for a gold coin, they will definitely spend it all. They regard it as improper to put the change in their pocket and leave. In other words, this is their manner of showing their grandiosity to the common people. But their grand patronage consists of treating each other to a cup of coffee, of impressing their friends with one cup of something four cups of which costs one *para* [penny].[5]

So popular were coffee houses in Istanbul that it was claimed that in 1564, ten years after the first establishments opened, there were over fifty in operation; by 1595 this number had supposedly reached six hundred.[6] It seems likely that this figure involved some conflation of coffee houses with taverns and *boza* outlets, which may also have reflected the reality of establishments blurring the boundaries between activities. Coffee houses allowed the consumption of dubious substances and opportunities for gaming and gambling, while the 'beautiful boys' employed as waiters were suspected of satisfying desires other than for caffeine. By 1565 Suleiman the Magnificent, the sultan who had welcomed the first coffee houses to Istanbul, was issuing edicts to close the taverns, *boza* sellers and coffee houses of Aleppo and Damascus, where people 'continue to pass their time by amusing themselves and committing illicit and banned acts' that prevented them 'from carrying out their religious obligations'.[7] Further and more severe edicts were issued by his successors, Selim II (1566–74) and Murad III (1574–95).

These appear to have had limited impact, not least because the enforcing authorities and militia members were themselves usually patrons, and not infrequently proprietors, of these institutions. The coffee houses' success reflected a shift in the social and political structures of the Ottoman Empire. The centralized, hierarchical administration model gave way to a society in which power was fragmented, elites divided and religious and secular ideologies contested. The coffee house, where one could address anyone directly and engage in open conversation, became a symbol of this new culture.

Coffee houses were attacked by religious and political conservatives precisely because of their progressive connotations. Sultan Murad IV, who came to the throne in 1623 when still a minor, had great difficulty establishing his authority, and instituted a highly reactionary regime complete with networks of informers stalking the coffee shops and listening for gossip against him. In 1633, following a fire that destroyed five districts in Istanbul and was believed to have been started by the smoking of tobacco in a coffee house, Murad ordered the closure of all such establishments in the city. Orders were despatched to other cities in the empire, like the municipality of Eyüp, that

> required that, with the arrival of this order, persons are sent to destroy any coffee kilns that are in the zone that you govern, and that from now on no one should be permitted to open one. From now on anyone who opens a coffee shop should be strung up over its front door.[8]

Although the use of tobacco, introduced into Turkey at the turn of the seventeenth century, seems to have been the primary target, or pretext, for Murad's wrath (he is reputed to have stalked the city in disguise at night, exacting summary justice upon offenders), the problem for coffee shop owners, as one *pasha* pointed out, was that

> In the coffee shops, the proprietors don't have the means to impose that customers, many of whom are soldiers, don't smoke; each one has his own tobacco in his pockets, he takes it out and smokes. Because (the smokers) have the privileges of state office holders, the proprietors of the coffee shops and the other inhabitants of the city cannot oppose them.[9]

Amedeo Preziosi, *A Turkish Coffee-house, Constantinople*, 1854, pencil and watercolour. Preziosi lived in Istanbul for forty years. The fireplace for preparing the coffee can be seen in the back left-hand corner, surrounded by coffee-making equipment. A Persian merchant serves coffee to his companion close to the fire, and a *finjan* and its metal holder can be seen on the seat in the front right of the picture. Most of the patrons preferred to smoke, however.

Terraced coffee fields near Manakhah, Yemen. Yemeni villages in the highlands are surrounded by terraced plots, some of which are planted as coffee groves. The cherries are dried on the flat roofs of the village.

The prohibition of coffee houses within Istanbul was still in place in the mid-1650s, though beyond the city walls coffee houses were trading openly, as they had probably continued to do in the empire's further regions throughout this period. By the last quarter of the seventeenth century, coffee houses had also reappeared in Istanbul, and travellers to the Ottoman territories remarked on the centrality of coffee houses in locations including Cairo's street markets, the caravan routes through the Arabian Peninsula and Istanbul's public gardens.

The spread of coffee throughout the Islamic world created a complex of long-distance trading networks that converged on Cairo, from where it was forwarded throughout the Ottoman Empire and eventually into Europe. Initially, wild coffee from Ethiopia was dried and shipped from Zeila (now in northern Somalia on the border with Djibouti). Here it would be added to the cargoes of spices originating in India and the Far East, carried up the Red Sea and offloaded at ports serving those regions where coffee had been adopted. The first coffee cargo mentioned comes in 1497 as part of a merchant's spice shipment from Tur at the Sinai peninsula's southern tip.[10]

Ethiopia remained the sole source of coffee until the 1540s, but a combination of rising demand and unreliable supplies due to conflicts between the African empire's Christian north and Muslim south led to coffee being cultivated in the highlands of the Yemeni interior between the coastal plain of Tihama and the capital city of Sana'a. Seeds from the small bean varieties found wild in Ethiopia were planted by peasants alongside subsistence crops on their family plots. These were the world's first coffee farms. The region remained the only centre of commercial coffee production for virtually two centuries. Villages of whitewashed stucco houses appeared throughout the mountains, surrounded by stone wall terraced plantations which were enriched with soil retrieved from the *wadis* following the rainy season. By the 1700s, these upland areas supported a population of some 1.5 million people.

The chain linking these producers to the final consumer was, as ever, a long and fragmented one. Transportation was exceptionally difficult, with nothing more than mule paths connecting mountainous areas to lowland markets. Growers would bring their dried cherries to the nearest town to exchange them for goods like cloth and salt. The coffee would then pass through various intermediaries before ending up in the major wholesale market of Bayt al-Faqih located on the coastal plain. Here it was bought by merchants and held in warehouses, prior to being transported by camel train to the ports of Al-Makha (otherwise known as Al-Mocha, Al-Mokka and, to Europeans, Mocha) and Hudaydah for shipping. Most of these merchants were Banyans, members of a diaspora that spread from the Gujarat port of Surat to dominate trade around the Indian Ocean. They also controlled the Yemeni credit networks, making it likely they were the chief financiers, and effective initiators, of coffee cultivation.

Despite its fragmented nature, the coffee trade generated considerable revenue, particularly among the leaders of the Zaydi sects who commanded the loyalty of the interior tribes. This facilitated considerable resistance to Ottoman rule. They were forced out from Yemen in 1638 by the Qasimi dynasty of Zaydi imams, who united the country for the first time and gained control over Zeila, thus giving them an effective monopoly over the world's coffee supply from both Yemen and Ethiopia. Beans from both origins subsequently became known within the trade as 'Mocha', as they were exported together from the same port.

The success of the Zaydi uprising led to a reorganization of the Red Sea trade. Coffee destined for consumption within the empire was transported by dhow from Hudaydah to Jeddah. This was established as an obligatory entrepôt by the Ottomans, who used the generated revenue to support the holy places. Ships bringing down cereals from Suez returned loaded with coffee for Cairo. Here the city's merchants, who had begun regularly trading coffee as early as the 1560s, would despatch it to the empire's major Mediterranean centres such as Salonika, Istanbul and Tunis. After the 1650s, coffee was sent to Alexandria, where it was acquired by the Marseille traders who controlled access to western European ports.

Mocha meanwhile acted as the principal port to the rest of the coffee-consuming world – primarily the Islamic lands surrounding the Persian Gulf, Arabian Sea and Indian Ocean. As a result, it also became the leading entrepôt for Indian commerce throughout the Red Sea. The British East India Company opened a depot there as early as 1618 to get a stake in the trade, forwarding consignments of what was variously described as 'cowa', 'cowhe', 'cowha', 'cohoo', 'couha' and 'coffa' on to company factors (brokers) in Persia and Moghul India, over thirty years before coffee became available in Britain. Although European companies managed to divert a significant portion of the spice trade into their own hands during the seventeenth century as exchanges between Europe and Indochina increased, coffee remained largely concentrated within the Muslim mercantile networks.

Olfert Dapper, 'Port of Al-Makha', 1680. Dapper's engraving was based on the accounts of merchants and missionaries. The Dutch flag is seen flying over a Dutch East India Company (voc) ship in the foreground, as well as over the voc factory visible on the shore to the left.

Part of the problem for the Europeans was the continuing unpredictability of supply. The agriculture structure in the Yemeni highlands made it difficult for growers to respond to market demands. Jean de la Roque – author, traveller and son of the merchant who introduced coffee to Marseille – wrote accounts of two trading expeditions to Mocha from the Breton port of St Malo, in 1709 and 1711. These reveal it took six months to fill the ship's hold, even though the Frenchmen were using a Banyan broker, whose attempts to acquire beans on their behalf drove up the prices in Bayt al-Faqih. A Dutch factor they encountered reckoned on taking a year to acquire cargo for one voyage. By the 1720s, Red Sea coffee shipments had reached 12,000–15,000 tonnes per annum – effectively the world supply.[11] That volume remained largely unchanged over the next hundred years, even though by 1840 it accounted for no more than 3 per cent of world production. Given this, it is hardly surprising that, as they increasingly adopted the beverage, Europeans sought to establish alternative cultivation centres.

After the 1720s, the Dutch turned to Java and the French to the Caribbean, so their purchases from Mocha and Alexandria, respectively, declined. These were compensated by increased purchases by the British and the Americans. The revenues from the coffee trade were still such that Muhammad Ali, the expansionist ruler of Egypt, sought to conquer Yemen to bring them under his control. This led the British to seize Aden in 1839, protecting their influence in the region, and establishing it as a free port in 1850. The absence of customs duties and the presence of deep-water quays and warehousing facilities saw Aden overtake Mocha as the region's chief coffee port. Today the harbour area of Mocha houses a small fishing fleet and many ruins, and is approached through silted-up channels, supposedly the consequence of nineteenth-century

American ships discharging their ballast prior to taking coffee on board.

The main causes of decline within the Red Sea coffee economy were changes in taste among the overwhelmingly Muslim consumers. It was the turn to tea in India and Iran in the early nineteenth century that had the most dramatic impact, as these traditional Eastern markets were lost to coffee. In Egypt, tea was likely the more popular beverage, made from plants cultivated within the country. Part of Ataturk's programme for Turkey's modernization during the twentieth century's first half was converting it into a tea-drinking country, substituting a beverage made from locally grown produce for an expensive import. It has taken the arrival of the Western coffee chains to stimulate a revival in Turkish coffee house culture.

Conversely, the one country where the coffee economy expanded over the last two centuries was Ethiopia. During the latter nineteenth century, Emperor Menelik used coffee export earnings to purchase firearms that were famously employed to defeat the Italians at Adowa in 1896, preserving Ethiopia's position as the lone independent African state after the continent's partition. As well as the 'wild' coffee from the southwest Oromo kingdoms such as Sidamo, Kaffa and Jimmah (probably produced on peasant plots to meet imperial demands for tribute), new plantations were established near the eastern region of Harar using cultivars of *Coffea arabica* that had evolved in growing areas around the world. These larger beans became known as Mocha Longberry, to distinguish them from the original Yemeni (and Ethiopian) 'Mocha'.

Coptic Christians in the north began to grow and consume coffee. The young Haile Selassie relied on coffee revenues to impose his authority in the 1930s. He, however, was unable to prevent the Italian Fascist occupation whose legacy includes the espresso bars of Addis Ababa and Asmara. Ethiopia remains one of the few growing countries that also consumes a significant portion (around 50 per cent) of its own coffee.

Jean-Étienne Liotard, *A Dutch Girl at Breakfast*, *c.* 1756, oil on canvas. By the middle of the 18th century coffee with milk and sugar was a standard breakfast beverage among the European bourgeoisie. The coffee pot shown here is known as a *dröppelminna*. Hot water was added to ground coffee in the pot, and the infusion delivered through the spout at the bottom. However, this was liable to clog with grounds, leading to the coffee dripping out, hence the name.

3
Colonial Good

Few Europeans, except those under Ottoman rule, had tasted coffee before the middle of the seventeenth century. Its introduction into Europe led to the creation of the coffee house and café, whose appeal extended to large swathes of European society. The eighteenth century witnessed a dramatic reconfiguration of coffee's production centres as European states, such as the Dutch Republic, France and Britain, began growing coffee in their Asian and Caribbean colonial holdings to satisfy consumers' increasing demand.

Diffusion of Coffee Culture in Europe

This was not a straightforward story of Europeans being bowled over by the bean. Chocolate, coffee and tea came to the continent in quick succession, and consumer preferences shifted back and forth. Guild regulation complexities prevented traders from setting up premises to sell and serve coffee. Consequently, there were significant discontinuities in the diffusion of coffee culture. Venice was probably the first European city in which coffee was brewed, but a coffee house did not open there until a century afterwards. London

Diffusion of Coffee Culture in Europe[1]

	First Record of Coffee in Territory	First Commercial Shipment Received	First Coffee House Opened	First Colonial Plantings
Italian States	1575 Venice	1624 Venice	1683 Venice	
Netherlands	1596 Leiden 1616 Amsterdam	1640 Amsterdam	1665 Amsterdam 1670 The Hague	1696 Java 1712 Suriname
England	1637 Oxford	1657 London	1650? Oxford 1652 London	1730 Jamaica
France	1644 Marseilles	1660 Marseilles	1670 Marseilles 1671 Paris	1715 Reunion 1723 Martinique
German States		1669 Bremen	1673 Bremen 1721 Berlin	
Habsburg Empire	1665 Vienna		1685 Vienna	

was home to Europe's first coffee houses, yet the British were among the last and the least active of the European coffee producers. Conversely the French, late converts from chocolate, went on to dominate both consumption and colonial production during the eighteenth century.

Coffee's adoption across Christian Europe reflected the continent's complex relationship with the Islamic Near East. Outbreaks of fascination with the 'Orient' provoked interest in coffee, yet travellers writing in the early seventeenth century often sought to rescue the beverage from its Muslim associations by reimagining its past. The Italian Pietro della Valle suggested coffee was the basis of nepenthe, the stimulant prepared by Helen in Homer's *Odyssey*. The Englishman Sir Henry Blount claimed it was the Spartans' black broth drunk before battles. By locating coffee among the ancient Greeks, they effectively claimed it for European civilization, and reminded contemporaries of coffee-drinking Christians within the Ottoman borders. There is, though, no evidence that Pope Clemente VIII tasted coffee and baptized it as a Christian beverage in the 1600s, although the story's widespread circulation suggests those with a stake in the coffee trade wished he had done so.

Coffee was present in Venice in 1575, as the coffee-making equipment recorded in the inventory of a murdered Turkish merchant in the city confirmed. By 1624 it was being shipped into the city for sale by apothecaries as a medicinal product, and in 1645 a shop selling beans appears to have been licensed.[2] Coffee's use spread to other Italian states: Tuscany awarded a monopoly for trading in coffee in 1665. Regulations protecting the apothecary trade probably account for the late appearance of the first café allowed to serve coffee in Venice in 1683. By 1759 the city authorities were forced to cap the number of cafés at 204 – a limit breached within four years.

It seems likely that similar restrictions obscured coffee's early history in the Habsburg Empire, particularly in territories bordering on, and often invaded by, the Ottomans. A Turkish delegation despatched to Vienna in 1665 to ratify a peace treaty included two men charged with coffee preparation. By 1666, when the delegation left, there was supposedly a thriving domestic coffee trade. It was dominated by Armenians, such as Johannes Diodato, who in 1685 was awarded the first licence for preparing and selling coffee – that is, operating a coffee house.[3]

This contradicts the embroidered story that Georg Franz Kolschitzky, a spy behind Ottoman lines during the 1683 siege of Vienna, had obtained the sacks of coffee beans abandoned by the retreating Turks as his reward, and used them to introduce coffee into the city. Supposedly Kolschitzky, in Turkish

This representation of Kolschitzky wearing Turkish dress while serving coffee in the Blue Bottle Coffee House was produced around 1900, feeding the myths surrounding his supposed introduction of coffee into Vienna.

dress, started by hawking pre-brewed coffee around the city, while petitioning authorities to be allowed to open his own shop. When that was granted, he set up the famous coffee house at the sign of the Blue Bottle. In 1697, three years after Kolschitzky's death, the licensed guild Bruderschaft der Kaffeesieder (Brotherhood of Coffeemakers) was established.[4] Their key innovation was adding milk to the coffee, with customers using a colour chart to indicate their desired shade. This was the origin of the *Kapuziner*, a beverage the colour of the Capuchin monks' tunic. As well as sweetening (or perhaps masking) the taste, milk symbolically transformed the black Muslim brew into a white Christian confection.

England evolved the first European coffee house culture. The leading figures in bringing the bean to Britain were also émigrés from the Ottoman Empire. Nathaniel Conopios, a

Greek student at Balliol College, Oxford, was the first person recorded drinking coffee in England in May 1637. A Jewish manservant from the Levant named Jacob has sometimes been credited with opening a coffee house in the same city in 1650, but, if he existed, he probably served, rather than sold, coffee to his master's companions. There is no doubt, however, that Pasqua Rosee, an ethnic Armenian from the Ottoman city of Smyrna (now Izmir) opened London's, and Europe's, first documented coffee house sometime between 1652 and 1654. Such was the new institution's swift take-off, there were 82 coffee-house keepers registered in 1663 with the City of London authorities.

Rosee's business began as a stall in St Michael's churchyard in the heart of the City of London, the independent borough at the metropolis's centre that contained most of London's financial and commercial institutions. Merchants would come from the nearby Royal Exchange to continue conversations while sipping coffee under the awning of Rosee's stall. According to the first reference to the business, in 1654, it served 'a Turkish-kind of drink made of water and some berry or Turkish-beane (that was) somewhat hot and unpleasant (but had) a good after relish and caused some breaking of wind in abundance'.[5]

A handbill extolled *The Vertue of the Coffee drink. First publiquely made and sold in England by Pasqua Rosee.* Coffee, it observed, was 'a simple innocent thing' prepared by being

> ground to Powder and boiled up with Spring water, and about a half pint of it to be drunk . . . as hot as possibly can be endured . . . It will prevent Drowsiness and make one fit for business, if one have occasion to Watch and therefore you are not to Drink of it after Supper, unless you intend to be watchful, for it will hinder sleep for 3 or

> 4 hours. It is observed in Turkey, where this is generally drunk, that they are not troubled with the Stone, Gout, Dropsie or Scurvey, and their Skins are exceedingly clear and white. It is neither Laxative nor Restringent.[6]

The beverage's principal benefit was the physiological effect of 'promoting watchfulness'. The advantage over drinking the 'small beer', or weak ale – the traditional form of refreshment in a city where water supplies were often filthy – can easily be gauged. The coffee house quickly took over from the tavern as the principal public venue in which to conduct business.

Local tavern-keepers resented Rosee's success, which they complained was stealing their business; but as he was not trading in alcohol, they were unable to argue that he was infringing on their licences. Instead they challenged his right to trade on the grounds that he was not a citizen, resulting in Rosee entering into partnership with Christopher Bowman, a member of the Company of Grocers. Together they transferred the enterprise into a set of rooms overlooking the churchyard. It continued trading under a sign of Rosee's silhouette, known as the Turk's Head, although there is no record of his being involved in the business beyond 1658. Bowman died in 1662, after which his widow took over until the premises were destroyed in the Great Fire of 1666.

It was no accident that coffee houses were established during the Cromwellian era following the English Civil War's end. The guilds' power weakened and the prevalent cultural values of egalitarianism and sobriety suited the introduction of an alcohol-free venue for socializing in which customers were treated as equals. Early proprietors installed long tables, seating everyone and anyone without a suggestion of hierarchy. The coffee was brewed over a fire and decanted into

Thomas Rowlandson, 'A Mad Dog in a Coffee House', 1809. This satirical print captures many features of the London coffee houses, though it was produced long after their heyday. A voluptuous hostess (the only woman present) presides behind the circular bar. The coffee pots stacked on the ledge to the left resemble Turkish *cezve*. Notices from shipping and stock brokers are posted on the wall on the right. The mad dog may have been part of an entertaining spectacle for clients.

coffee pots, from which waiters poured it into bowls – known as dishes – for the customers.

Coffee houses survived the monarchy's restoration in 1660 because Royalist opponents of the Parliamentary regime had also taken advantage of the opportunities these venues created for unmonitored conversation. When the Earl of Clarendon proposed to the Privy Council in 1666 closing down coffee houses, he was reminded by William Coventry that 'in Cromwell's time . . . the King's friends had used more liberty of Speech in these Places than They durst do in any other'.[7] That was true in Oxford where the first documented coffee house outside the capital was opened by apothecary Arthur Tillyard in 1656. Tillyard was 'encouraged to do so by some royalists, now living in Oxon, and by others who esteemed themselves either virtuosi or wits'.[8]

The term 'virtuosi' described gentlemen possessed of intellectual curiosity about cultural novelties, rarities and the fledgling field of empirical, quasi-scientific enquiry associated with figures such as Francis Bacon. As virtuosi were not courtiers, they were free to learn about new phenomena and discuss them within the so-called 'penny universities' – the price coffee houses charged for a dish of coffee.

Tillyard's customers included Issac Newton, the father of modern physics, the astronomer Edmond Halley (of comet fame) and the collector Hans Sloane, whose bequest formed the basis of the British Museum. Most of the virtuosi were not such outstanding scholars but enthusiasts who could be enticed into coffee houses to inspect displays of curiosities. Don Saltero's coffee house, opened in London in 1729 by James Salter, included attractions like 'Painted Ribbands from Jerusalem with the Pillar to which our Saviour was tied when scourged' and 'A large Snake 17-foot-long, taken in a pigeon house in Sumatra, it had in its belly 15 fowls and 5 pigeons'.[9]

Other great patrons of coffee houses were City businessmen, who congregated in certain establishments to conduct their affairs. The most well known are Lloyd's, founded in 1688, which became the centre for maritime insurance, and Jonathan's, whose role as a rudimentary stock exchange saw it play a leading role in the South Sea Bubble, the frenzied share speculation and subsequent market crash, of 1711. The value of networking at the coffee house was recognized by Samuel Pepys, who took the decision to frequent them over taverns in 1663, drinking coffee until he 'was almost sick', but acquiring considerable wealth from the kick-backs on his naval supply deals.[10]

A distinction needs to be drawn between the success of the coffee houses and that of coffee. Chocolate and tea were available as alternative beverages within the coffee houses as early as 1660. In 1664 the Grecian coffee house, home to the newly founded Royal Society, advertised that it not only sold chocolate and tea but offered customers lessons in how to make them. Tellingly, a second aborted attempt by King Charles's ministers to suppress coffee houses in 1675 defined them as any house selling 'Coffee, Chocolate, Sherbett, or Tea'. The fact that Whites, the first 'chocolate house', was only founded in 1693, and Thomas Twining opened his original teahouse in 1711, is not so much an indication of the later take-up of these beverages as of their earlier availability.

Coffee's association with the coffee house may have held back its adoption in the home. The coffee house was essentially a male environment in which talking to strangers was encouraged. The only women present were either serving or 'servicing' the customer's needs. The *Women's Petition against Coffee* – a 1674 condemnation of both coffee and coffee houses on the grounds that they kept men away from the home and rendered them impotent – was probably sponsored by brewers keen to recapture lost customers, but it played on this gender division.

Well-bred women were directed towards tea. Tea was favoured by several royal role models, notably the Portuguese Catherine of Braganza, who introduced it to the English court in 1662 when she married Charles II. Subsequently England was ruled by two sovereign queens, Mary (1688–94) and her sister Anne (1702–14), both of whom were tea drinkers. Women might take tea together, either at home, or publicly in tea gardens where the open-air settings conferred a visibility, rendering them respectable places for ladies.

It is difficult to gauge the full extent of London's coffee house explosion. The next apparently accurate figures are from Henry Maitland, whose exhaustive survey of the capital in 1739 revealed 551 coffee houses – around one per thousand head of population. In the City borough alone, 144 coffee houses were recorded – a number roughly equal to taverns and inns. The 8,000-plus gin palaces Maitland also identified in London, outnumbering coffee houses by some eighty to one in the poorest quarters of the capital, were, however, an indication of coffee's elite beverage status. Tea consumption began to permeate into the lower classes after the 1740s. Tariffs were cut on the Chinese tea imported by the British East India Company, but coffee bought on the international market continued to incur heavy duties.

In the second half of the eighteenth century coffee houses began to offer alcohol alongside coffee, effectively turning back into taverns, as the number of pubs with names like The Turk's Head indicates. One example was The Turk's Head in Gerrard Street, London, which hosted a literary club in 1764. Members included the great lexicographer Dr Samuel Johnson and his biographer James Boswell. They drank tea and wine respectively. Some coffee houses doubled as bordellos, as seen in Hogarth's 1738 picture *Morning*, depicting King's Coffee House in London's Covent Garden. Those hosting business activities at times turned into exchanges themselves (Lloyd's), while meeting places for the virtuosi increasingly became private gentlemen's clubs to preserve societal distinction. A commercial guide to London published in 1815 listed just twelve coffee houses.

This contrasted with the French café, which, though slower to become established, developed into a social institution appealing to all classes during the eighteenth century. Coffee was traded in Marseilles by the 1640s but remained largely unknown in Paris until 1669. In that year a diplomatic mission was sent by Sultan Mehmed IV to Louis XIV, probably instigated by the French ambassador to Constantinople to impress his own sovereign. The delegation remained for almost a year, entertaining influential courtiers with Turkish delicacies like coffee in a mansion refurbished as a Persian palace. This inspired 'Turkomania' among French society's upper echelons, as satirized in Molière's *Le Bourgeois gentilhomme*. Vendors started selling coffee during trade fairs in the Saint-Germain commercial district, and an Armenian named Pascal established the first Parisian coffee house in 1671, only to see it fail after this Turkish fad subsided.

It was not until the early 1700s that a long-running dispute between the guilds of the *limonadiers* (distillers), grocers and apothecaries over the right to sell coffee was finally resolved. The *limonadiers* were granted an effective monopoly over the service of decoctions – be they lemonade, coffee or gin – to seated customers on their premises. This created the café format as an establishment in which coffee and alcohol were taken – often with the intention of using the properties of the former to counteract those of the latter.

An early example was the Café Procope, established in 1686 by the Italian-born *limonadier* Francesco Procopio, who renamed himself François Procope. It was furnished with gilded mirrors, marble tables, painted ceilings and chandeliers, recalling an aristocratic salon rather than a sultan's seraglio. Coffee and its accompaniments were served using porcelain tableware and silver cutlery. Located across from the newly founded Comédie Française, its elite patrons could enjoy encountering theatrical performers, while feeling safe in their surroundings. The Procope became the model for the grand cafés throughout eighteenth-century Europe, such as Florian's in Venice and Caffè Greco in Rome.

Artist unknown, the Café Procope, Paris, around 1700.

By 1720 there were in the region of 280 cafés in Paris, rising to around 1,000 in 1750 and 1,800 in 1790, serving a population of approximately 650,000. Most of these catered to more modest clienteles than the Procope, providing Parisians with venues for meeting and socializing, playing games such as chequers, or gambling on the various lotteries. Clay pipes were kept ready loaded for the use of customers, as smoking tobacco was almost ubiquitous. The fittings and furnishings were matched to the clienteles' social station, while cafés seeking extra space spilled onto the boulevards. Locations immediately outside city limits had lower rents, offering customers access to pastoral pleasures during the day, and the demi-monde by night.

The café was part of the masculine world. Although many cafés were run by couples, with the woman working front of house while her male partner prepared the drinks and accompaniments in the backroom 'laboratory', few women set foot in a café for fear of being mistaken as prostitutes due to the café's public nature and its trade in alcohol. If women were served coffee, it was likely taken to their carriage to be drunk in privacy.

Bourgeois women chose chocolate, not least for its supposedly medicinal qualities. Coffee began to challenge this primacy with the spread of *café au lait*. As Philippe Dufour explained in his 1684 book on coffee, tea and chocolate, 'when [ground] coffee is boiled in milk and a little thickened, it approaches the flavour of chocolate which nearly everyone finds good.'[11] Furthermore, *café au lait* could be presented as French rather than foreign in origin. As an enthusiastic noblewoman states in 1690, 'We have here good milk and good cows; we've taken it into our heads to skim the cream . . . and mix it with sugar and good coffee.'[12]

The Low Countries witnessed an even more rapid adoption of coffee among both sexes and throughout the classes. Coffee-making equipment was frequently found among probate inventories of lower-class and middling households in eighteenth-century Amsterdam. As early as 1726 it was claimed coffee 'has broken through so generally in our land that maids and seamstresses now have to have their coffee in the morning or they cannot put their thread through the eye of their needle'.[13] It seems weavers, undertaking piecework within their homes, were fuelling themselves with sugar-sweetened coffee to avoid leaving their looms.

Coffee's growing popularity led European trading companies to try and secure supplies: the situation became acute in 1707 when the Ottoman administration imposed an export ban on coffee outside the empire. By then Nicolaes Witsen, a governor of the Dutch East India Company (voc), had already started to plant coffee on Java in 1696. The seeds came from Malabar in India, where legend has it that coffee was planted by the Muslim scholar Baba Budan, who smuggled the seeds back in his clothing following a pilgrimage to Mecca. A more likely explanation for the presence of coffee in Malabar was that this was an outgrowth of the Banyan coffee trade.

On Java, the VOC operated by coercing indigenous chiefs into supplying a fixed quantity of coffee in exchange for a low, pre-established, price. Local lords required peasant households under their control to provide them with coffee as part of their feudal obligations. Coffee was a crop that conferred neither financial nor nutritional value to themselves, so the peasants had little incentive to improve cultivation techniques. They preferred to meet quotas by growing coffee in their domestic plots or forest gardens. Peasant households in western Java, where cultivation was concentrated, were at times forced to relocate to locations suitable for growing coffee in plantations, under the control of the lord's subordinates.[14]

Regular shipments from Java to Holland began in 1711, enabling Amsterdam to establish the first European coffee exchange. In 1721, 90 per cent of the coffee on the Amsterdam market originated in the Yemen; by 1726, 90 per cent was supplied from Java.[15] Deliveries from the island continued to increase until the middle of the century, but tailed off as new plantations in the Caribbean took over.

The Dutch were partly responsible for this. In 1712 they introduced coffee to Suriname, a colonial enclave on the northeastern coastline of mainland Latin America, bordering the Caribbean Sea. Exports began in 1721 and surpassed those from Java by the 1740s. In Suriname, cultivators had no option but to produce coffee – the crop was grown on plantations tended by slave labour.

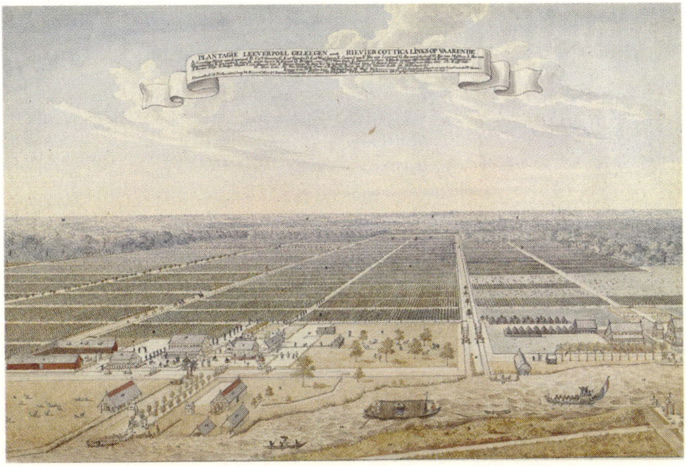

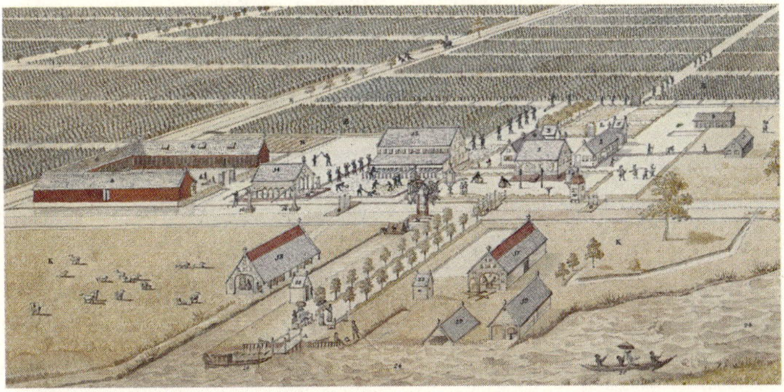

View of the Leeverpoel coffee plantation in Suriname, *c.* 1700–1800. This remarkable anonymous drawing shows the scale of the coffee plantation. The main buildings are situated immediately behind the landing area and sluice. In the bottom image, on the left is the three-sided slave housing bloc with small allotments behind. To the right is the processing area where workers can be seen raking coffee on a patio and drying it on raised tables. The plantation director and overseers live in the 'white' housing, as it is labelled, on the centre-right, with their leisure gardens to the far right.

In 1715 the French planted coffee on the island of Bourbon (now Réunion), part of the Mauritanian archipelago off Africa's east coast. In the 1640s the French East India Company had begun colonizing the uninhabited island, granting concessions of land to French settlers who worked them with African slaves. Arabica trees obtained from Yemen, in defiance of the Ottoman ban, proved so successful that the Company decreed in 1724 that it would repossess any concessions that failed to plant coffee, and even debated imposing the death penalty for deliberately damaging a coffee tree.[16]

In the 1720s the French also introduced coffee to their Caribbean territories, starting with Martinique. Gabriel de Clieu, a young naval officer, supposedly transported cuttings of coffee plants from Paris's botanic gardens to the island in 1723, many years later publishing a heroic account of how he shared his water ration with them during the voyage. It now seems that planting began in 1724 using seeds from Bourbon and Suriname.

When and how coffee arrived on Saint Domingue (now Haiti) is less clear, but its success soon outstripped production everywhere else in the Caribbean. The French obtained the colony at the end of the Nine Years War in 1697 when Hispaniola was divided into two. Santo Domingo, the eastern portion (today's Dominican Republic) remained under Spanish control, while Saint Domingue occupied the rugged western third of the island. As elsewhere in the Caribbean, the lower coastal areas were devoted to sugar-cane plantations, while coffee farms were established in the mountainous interior.

Up until the 1730s, the French East India Company refused to allow coffee grown in either Bourbon or the Caribbean to be sold in France. This was to protect its own monopoly on the more highly priced Mocha. Instead, coffee from these origins was shipped to the Amsterdam exchange

A woman selling *café au lait*, from Adrien Joly's *Arts, metiers et cris de Paris* (1826 edn).

– including *café marron*, a coffee species now known as Mauritian coffee (*Coffea mauritiana*) found growing wild on Bourbon. It proved inferior to the cultivated Arabica and was abandoned in the 1720s. By the 1750s, the proportion of coffee from the Americas traded on the Amsterdam exchange matched that from Asia.

The influx of colonial coffee into France after the import ban was lifted in the mid-seventeenth century drove down the price and made the beverage more accessible to the lower classes. A degree of snobbery developed around coffee-drinking styles, with the philosopher Jacques-François Demachy drawing a comparison in 1775 between

> a woman of high society, comfortably settled in her armchair, who consumes a succulent breakfast to which mocca has added its perfume for a well-varnished tea table, in a . . . gilded porcelain cup, with well-refined sugar and good cream; and . . . a vegetable seller soaking a bad penny loaf in a detestable liquor, which she has been told is Café au Lait, in a ghastly earthenware pot.[17]

By the 1780s, 80 per cent of the world's coffee supply came from the Caribbean, principally Saint Domingue. More plantations were established between the 1760s and 1780s, until the value of coffee exports matched those of sugar cane. The colony's success lay in the low costs of production – achieved principally with imported African slave labour.

A remarkable, if disturbing, guide to coffee growing in Saint Domingue was published by the planter P. J. Laborie in 1798. He described all the stages of coffee cultivation, from clearing the land to bagging the beans. The book includes an account of the innovative 'West Indian process' for pulping the cherries, using a water-channels system to soften the fruit and pass it through a series of graters. Yet what leaps out is his belief that 'the negroe' (his term for slaves) 'is that creature that we are forced to keep in his natural state of thraldom to obtain from him the requisite services; because . . . under a different condition he would not labour'.[18]

When buying slaves, Laborie advised looking for features such as an open cheerful countenance, a clean and lively eye, sound teeth, sinewy arms, dry and large hands, strong loins and haunches, and an easy and free movement of the limbs. After purchase, they were forced to drink 'sudorific potions' for a fortnight to sweat out diseases picked up on the voyage, and the 'unpleasant but necessary' act of branding them was performed.

New slaves had to be 'seasoned' – introduced gradually into farm work as they assimilated to the cooler climate. Laborie preferred to buy young boys and girls of around fifteen who could be formed to 'the Master's own ideas' while undertaking gardening and weeding. They would then join the main gang, working on the plantation from sunrise to sunset, under the authority of a driver – an entrusted slave equipped with a whip.

Maintaining authority was a priority. Insubordination such as talking back to master or driver was more severely punished than any offence committed by one slave against another – including violent assaults and rape. Laborie wrote of the need to clean whips between floggings to avoid spreading infection.

Racial politics in Saint Domingue was complicated. Over a third of coffee plantations, and a quarter of all the slaves, were owned by so-called *gens de couleur*. This group comprised French settlers' mixed-race offspring recognized by their fathers, plus, a growing number of black former slaves, who had been freed by their masters. By 1789 the colony had

'La Marie-Séraphique', 1773. This anonymous watercolour shows the French slave ship registered in Nantes at anchor in the Cap Français harbour in Saint Domingue, at the end of its voyage from Angola. It is the opening day of the sale of its human cargo. The ship is divided by an iron barrier confining the slaves to the main deck, while the auction takes place on the quarter deck and the European purchasers enjoy a picnic on the stern.

28,000 *gens de couleur* and 30,000 whites, but both groups were 'outnumbered' by the 465,000 slaves.

The 1789 French revolution encouraged the *gens de couleur* to assert their rights to be treated as equal to the white population, while slaves used the instability to stage their own rebellions for better conditions. From 1791 these forces came together in an uneasy alliance led by Toussaint L'Ouverture, a freed black slave who had at one point owned a coffee plantation and fifteen slaves. A sickening cycle of violence, foreign intervention, repression and war lasted until 1804 when Saint Domingue declared its independence, renamed itself Haiti and abolished slavery. Over a thousand coffee plantations were destroyed, including that of Laborie, who fled to Jamaica. Although new farms were established, the coffee trade was effectively lost because European states and the USA shunned Haiti for fear of legitimizing black rule.

Within Europe, the coffee supply disruption was intensified by the British navy's blockade of French territories. Napoleon's response was to encourage home-grown chicory as a substitute. Chicory was also promoted by Frederick the Great in Prussia. He employed so-called 'coffee sniffers' in the 1780s to clamp down on consumption. The practice of bulking out the beans with roasted chicory became pervasive. Even in the early twentieth century, William Ukers, founding editor of the trade journal *Tea and Coffee*, complained that many Europeans had 'acquired a chicory and coffee taste such that is doubtful if they would appreciate a real cup of coffee should they ever meet it'.[19]

Nonetheless the first half of the nineteenth century saw a continued increase of coffee consumption throughout Europe. Swedish novels of the period feature scenes in which coffee is drunk by all classes: for example, in Emilie Flygare-Carlén's *Pål Värning*, published in 1844, the hero is a poor fisherman who makes a hazardous journey to buy coffee for his sick mother. At the tavern-cum-shop he encounters an elderly maid, for whom 'sitting by the kitchen stove with a pipe in her mouth, and with the coffee pot on the fire was . . . the finest pleasure in life'. Coffee came to be sold in 'Colonial Goods' shops – aptly named, as most European supplies still came from their imperial possessions.

The first drip-brewing apparatus appeared in the early nineteenth century, so-called de Belloy pots named after the coffee-loving Archbishop of Paris. A filter compartment containing the ground coffee separated two chambers, so that hot water poured into the upper could filter down into the lower. Later pots were designed so the water could be heated on the stove, then the apparatus flipped over to allow percolation to take place.[20] Over the course of the century, fashionable forms of equipment such as syphon systems and hydrostatic percolators found favour among the elite, while drip brewing became widespread across much of Europe.

The demise of Saint Domingue sparked a revival of coffee production in Asia. Java's popularity saw the island's name adopted as a synonym for coffee in the United States. However, what was sold as 'Java' was as likely to have originated in Sumatra and other Dutch colonies across the Indonesian archipelago. It could take five months for coffee to be shipped to New York, during which time the beans aged and often turned brown due to sweating. The coffee became prized for its low acidity, and continued to be shipped in sailing vessels even after the advent of steam.

The Dutch colonial authorities continued to work through local rulers, introducing the so-called Collection System that required peasant households to set aside a portion of their land or labour to cultivate commercial crops sold exclusively to the state. The autobiographical novel *Max Havelaar*, penned

Koffi, *c.* 1870s. This print was produced by the Kolff publishing company based in Batavia, the capital of the Dutch East Indies (now Jakarta in Indonesia). It shows the various stages of coffee picking, processing and preparation, although little of the coffee grown in these territories would have been consumed there, especially not in native households. The brewer shown is a version of the de Belloy pot, in which hot water is introduced to the upper chamber and percolates through a bed of ground coffee into the lower one. The presence of the milk jug further suggests this poster was for Dutch consumers.

by a former administrator in 1860, showed how peasants starved while the Dutch indulged their indigent lords.[21] By the 1880s, 60 per cent of Java's peasant households were forced to grow coffee. Tending to the trees took up 15 per cent of their time, yet generated only 4 per cent of their income, due to the low fixed prices.

The British also expanded their colonial coffee production, most notably on Ceylon (Sri Lanka). Having gained control of the coast from the Dutch during the Napoleonic Wars,

Coffee leaf rust. The telltale spots of rust are first found on the underside of the leaf.

they set about conquering the interior, overthrowing the independent Kingdom of Kandy in 1815. British entrepreneurs cleared the forests to set up coffee plantations, killing off many of the island's elephants and importing workers from the heavily indebted Tamil population of the Indian region of Madras. Untold numbers died 'on the road' to these plantations or due to working conditions when they got there.[22]

By the late 1860s total British coffee production in Ceylon and India was approaching that of the Dutch colonies. In 1869 an outbreak of leaf rust caused by the fungus *Hemileia vastatrix* began. By the mid-1880s the coffee plantations had been largely destroyed, and were converted to growing tea, cementing the triumph of leaf over bean in Britain. By 1913 Ceylon was a net coffee importer.

The rust outbreak spread throughout Asia, wiping out most of the production in Java, Sumatra and the rest of the East Indies, as well as India. It even travelled as far as Africa and the Pacific Islands. Some planters substituted Arabica trees with Liberia's native species, *Coffea liberica*. Its harsh-tasting beans found little favour, except among locals in Malaysia and the Philippines, where it became the basis for Barako, a dark-roasted, highly caffeinated coffee. In any case Liberica, too, proved susceptible to the fungus. By the outbreak of the First World War, Asia provided just one-twentieth of the world coffee supply, compared to around one-third before the rust appeared. The global coffee economy was now centred in the Americas.

Winslow Homer, 'The Coffee Call', 1863. In this print soldiers in the Army of the Potomac are shown queueing up for coffee prepared in large pails over a campfire.

4
Industrial Product

Coffee was transformed into an industrial product during the latter part of the nineteenth century by two nations in the Americas: Brazil and the United States. Brazil's ability to rapidly expand coffee output without significantly raising its prices enabled the U.S. to absorb this into its enlarging consumer economy. Brazil extended the coffee frontier into its hinterlands by replacing a slave labour force with imported European peasant labourers. U.S. consumption per capita tripled between the mid-nineteenth and mid-twentieth centuries, as consumers moved from home roasting to purchasing pre-prepared, branded industrial coffee products. Once Central America and Colombia began to compete for the U.S. market, new forms of coffee politics appeared, as states strove to protect their national interests.

Coffee in the USA: From the Colonial Era to the Civil War

Americans' preference for coffee is often presented as an outcome of the struggle for independence. Tea became a symbolic focus for the colonists' demands for 'no taxation

United States Coffee Consumption Statistics, 1880–1950[1]

Date	Total Imports (million lbs)	Consumption per Capita (lbs)	Share of World Imports (%)
1800	8.8	1.65	
1830	38.3	2.98	
1860	182.0	5.78	28.7
1890	490.1	8.31	36.1
1920	1,244.9	11.88	56.1
1950	2,427.7	16.04	63.6

without representation'. The British government imposed a duty on tea imports into the colonies, which were also part of an East India Company monopoly. Protestors staged the Boston Tea Party on 16 December 1773, tipping tea chests off ships in Chesapeake Bay harbour. Consequently, the story goes, American patriots switched to coffee.

The reality is more complicated. Coffee had long been available in the colonies; particularly in Boston, where Dorothy Jones became the first person licensed to sell 'coffee and cuchaletto [chocolate]' in 1670. Coffee houses spread through the city, mostly doubling as taverns: the Green Dragon, founded in 1697, was a regular meeting place for political activists. Coffee imports into the colonies were also controlled by the British, however, coming principally from Jamaica.

After the Tea Party, the patriotic response was to secure alternatives to British supplies. John Adams requested 'a Dish of Tea providing it has been honestly smuggled or paid no Duties' in 1774. In 1777, after his wife Abigail described how Bostonian women had broken into a warehouse in search of coffee and sugar, Adams hoped that 'females will leave off their attachment to coffee', and start drinking beverages made from American-grown products.[2]

Coffee gained popularity once French supplies from Saint Domingue began to arrive into the newly independent United States. By 1800 consumption was over 680 grams (1.5 lb) per capita.[3] The U.S. developed a lucrative re-export trade in coffee during the Napoleonic wars. Coffee from the Caribbean was carried to Europe in American vessels to avoid naval blockades.

After 1820 consumption increased significantly, sparked by a fall in prices from 21 cents a pound in 1821 to 8 cents in 1830. The cause of the fall was speculators hoarding coffee in anticipation of a Franco-Spanish war that didn't break out, leaving them to dump beans on the international market. As the world supply expanded, coffee prices rarely exceeded 10 cents per pound for the following two decades. The U.S. federal government removed import taxes on coffee in 1832, and by 1850 consumption was over 2.3 kilograms (5 lb) per capita.

Cuba became the United States' primary supplier following the demise of Saint Domingue, with many American investors acquiring plantations on the island. After a series of natural disasters destroyed hundreds of trees in the 1840s, however, many switched to sugar. Thereafter the U.S. increasingly obtained low-price coffee from Latin America, especially Brazil.

The Civil War (1860–65) was a pivotal event in the United States' coffee history. Union troops were plied with coffee: a daily ration of about 43 grams (1.5 oz) of coffee a day totalled a staggering 16 kilograms (36 lb) a year. That could easily support the consumption of ten cups of coffee a day. Generals, aware of caffeine's psychoactive effects, ensured their men had drunk plenty of coffee before battle; some soldiers carried grinders fitted into the butt of their rifles. The Union blockade

'McKinley's coffee run'. Detail from the memorial to future President McKinley's feat at the Antietam National Battlefield. It was erected in 1903, two years after his assassination.

of the Southern coastline meant the Confederate states – and their troops – were forced to use substitutes like chicory and acorns.

Coffee's centrality to the troops' existence can be gauged from the fact that the word 'coffee' appears more frequently in soldiers' diaries of the period than 'rifle', 'cannon' or 'bullet'. Sergeants distributing coffee rations avoided accusations of favouritism by facing the other way when calling up men to receive their allotment. John Billings, an artilleryman, in his memoir *Hardtack and Coffee*, described how dipping the former in the latter killed off the weevils in the biscuit as they floated to the surface. He recalled:

> If a march was ordered at midnight . . . it must be preceded by a pot of coffee; if a halt was ordered in mid-forenoon or afternoon, the same dish was inevitable. . . . It was coffee *at* meals and *between* meals . . . and today the old soldiers who can stand it are the hardest coffee drinkers in the community.[4]

The bloodiest day of the Civil War was 17 September 1862 at Antietam. Nineteen-year-old Sergeant William McKinley (later a U.S. president) passed along the front line serving the troops coffee, despite coming under heavy fire. The effect on morale 'was like putting a new regiment in the fight' according to their commanding officer.[5]

Foundations of the Coffee Industry

When Civil War soldiers returned home, their coffee-drinking habit stimulated the emerging domestic coffee industry. By the 1880s America was importing one-third of the world's coffee, occasioning the establishment of the New York Coffee Exchange in 1882.

Throughout the nineteenth century, most coffee in the largely rural U.S. was purchased in bulk as green beans from a catalogue supplier or general store. Batches of beans were roasted at home in a pan over a wood stove, stirred for around twenty minutes. Better-off households might have a sealed home roaster turned by hand or by steam. Home grinders were becoming common by mid-century, but the mortar and pestle were frequently used to crush roasted beans into powder.

Preparation techniques were simple – coffee grounds were heated with water in a kettle. Household guides recommended boiling for 20–25 minutes. A variety of additives were employed to encourage the grounds to settle to the bottom – most frequently egg white, but also isinglass (a fish-based gelatine product).

The first popular refinement was the Old Dominion coffee pot in 1859. This was an early percolator, in which coffee was placed in a perforated container within a lower chamber which boiled the water, while a condenser unit above liquefied and recycled escaping vapour. Users were advised to leave coffee and water in the pot on the stove overnight, then boil again for ten to fifteen minutes before breakfast. The thin-bodied yet bitter-tasting brew became the characteristic taste of American coffee.

By the 1840s the emergence of major urban centres created conditions for new wholesale coffee-roasting businesses. These supplied stores with loose, ready-roasted beans sold by

Carter pull-out roasters in operation in an early industrial coffee-roasting operation. Each cylinder held around 90 kg (200 lb) of coffee. Original print in Francis Thurber, *Coffee: From Plantation to Cup* (1887).

weight. Beans were roasted using the pull-out roaster patented by James W. Carter of Boston in 1846. This comprised a long roasting cylinder set into a brick-built furnace fired by coal. A pulley system drew the cylinder in and out of the furnace, and it was filled and emptied using sliding doors set in its sides.

Operators judged when coffee was ready from the colour of the smoke emitting around the cylinder's edges. They unloaded the hot coffee into trays then stirred the beans by hand until cool. Some simply dumped the hot coffee directly onto the floor, spreading it with rakes and sprinkling with water. One observer recalled how 'the contact of water and hot coffee caused so much steam that the roasting room was in a dense fog for several minutes after each batch of coffee was withdrawn from the fire'.[6]

In 1864 Jabez Burns patented his self-emptying roaster. Within the revolving cylinder set in a brick oven, a so-called 'double screw' allowed the beans to be moved uniformly up and down for an even roast. The key was that the beans could be emptied from the front, into a cooling tray, without taking the cylinder from the fire. Burns developed further refinements for cooling and grinding the coffee that saved time, significantly reducing the price difference between green and roasted coffee at wholesale and retail. In 1874 Burns declared:

> It is preposterous to suppose that household roasting will be continued long in any part of this country, if coffee properly prepared can be had . . . It will never pay for small stores to roast if the large manufactories do the work well . . . By doing the work with proper care they will not only secure . . . large sales for themselves, but will command the roasting for other parties.[7]

Coffee in the United States was set to become a mass-manufactured, industrial product – branded and marketed to an emergent consumer society.

The Rise of the Coffee Brands

John Arbuckle of Pittsburgh, who ran a wholesale grocery business with his brother, was one of the first purchasers of the new Burns machine. In 1865 he started selling roasted coffee in reinforced paper packaging (developed for peanuts). Three years later he patented an egg and sugar glaze for roasting, claiming it prevented the beans from staling by protecting the surface from air and clarifying the brew. His advertisements showed a woman roasting beans at a wood stove and lamenting, 'Oh, I have burnt my coffee again', and being advised by her well-dressed guest to 'Buy Arbuckles' Roasted, as I do, and you will have no trouble.' The text underneath stated, 'You cannot roast coffee properly yourself.'[8]

In 1873 Arbuckles launched Ariosa, which became the first nationally known coffee brand: glazed beans wrapped in a distinctive yellow packaging with Arbuckles in red, and a flying angel trademark design above the name. By 1881 the company was roasting with 85 Burns machines in New York and Pittsburgh factories, and had distribution depots in Chicago and Kansas.

Ariosa's most dedicated market was the cowboys, ranchers and pioneers in the Far West. Many were demobilized Civil War soldiers who had acquired a taste for coffee. Each pack contained a peppermint stick, the sweet taste of which was designed to offset that of the coffee. Wagon train cooks allegedly called 'Who wants the candy?' to entice volunteers to grind the beans. Each pack contained coupons that could

Arbuckles Ariosa coffee trade card.

be redeemed for items such as tools, guns, razors, curtains and even wedding rings. The angel image was used to persuade Native Americans that coffee could confer spiritual powers, experienced as a caffeine buzz.

The rise of wholesale coffee roasting saw the development of several other prominent brands. Jim Folger set up Folgers coffee roasting company in San Francisco during the 1850s Gold Rush. In 1878 Caleb Chase and James Sanborn merged their coffee companies, begun in Boston, and started the Seal brand – the first to use sealed cans for packing.

Canned coffee became the U.S. standard, although the process also sealed in air, so staling remained an issue. Hills Brothers, another San Francisco company, addressed this by introducing vacuum-packed coffee in 1900. This technology favoured pre-ground coffee, like Hills' top-of-the-range Red Can brand. In 1892 the Cheek-Neal company introduced Maxwell House – named after a swanky Nashville hotel that they supplied.

By 1915, 85 per cent of consumers preferred to purchase pre-packaged branded coffee over loose roasted beans. Some

3,500 brands existed, though not all were on local grocery stores' shelves. Around 60 per cent of the market was with door-to-door delivery companies: the largest, the Jewell Tea Company, earned half its income from coffee sales. Chain stores' own-brand coffee accounted for another significant market share. The Great Atlantic and Pacific Tea Company, commonly known as the A&P, sold their own brand Eight O'Clock Coffee – adding 'theatre' by installing in-store grinders.

Coffee cemented its position as America's national beverage during the early twentieth century as consumption reached 5 kilograms (11 lb) per capita. The United States now imported well over half of the world's coffee supply, and roasters positioned their brands as inherently American with names such as 'Buffalo' and 'Dining Car Special'. Thomas Wood & Co. boasted that its Uncle Sam's Coffee came from 'his own possessions in Porto Rico, Hawaii and Manilla [*sic*]'.

Chase & Sanborn's Seal Brand Java and Mocha – the first canned coffee. The brand name was shortened to Seal when regulations governing claims of provenance were tightened.

Most roasters were reticent about the origins of their blends, however. Hills Brothers trademarked the figure of an Arab in a flowing robe in 1897, using brand names like Caravan, Santola, Timingo and Saxon, which obscured more than they revealed. Java and Mocha remained the only acknowledged production sources, promoting cowboy slang for coffee – 'jamoka'. Arbuckles warned consumers to 'beware of buying low-grade package coffee falsely purporting to be made of Mocha, Java and Rio; this being a cheap device employed by the manufacturers to deceive unwary customers.'[9] Ariosa was widely presumed to be composed of beans from Rio and Santos. By the mid-1870s more than 75 per cent of the coffee consumed in the United States came from Brazil.

Coffee in Brazil

Coffee was supposedly introduced to the Portuguese colony by Francisco de Melo Palheta in 1727. The story goes that the diplomat Palheta was sent to resolve a dispute between Dutch and French colonies in Guiana. He returned to Brazil with seeds hidden in a bouquet from his lover, the French governor's wife. He planted them in Para, his home region, but until 1822 coffee remained a minor crop in Brazil compared to sugar.

Coffee's fortunes were transformed when it was introduced into the mountainous Paraiba valley region, south of Rio de Janeiro, in response to rising prices following the demise of Saint Domingue. Coffee trees took well to the *terra roxa* – the well-drained and nutrient-rich red clay soil found in Brazil's central-southern states.

Cultivation techniques were crude, with little regard for the environment. Hillside forests were cut and burnt down,

Brazilian Coffee Production Statistics, 1870–1990[10]

Date (two-year averages)	Brazilian Production (million sacks)	World Production (million sacks)	Share of World Production (%)
1870–71	3.1	6.6	46.9
1900–1901	14.5	18.7	77.5
1930–31	25.1	37.0	67.8
1960–61	32.9	68.9	47.7
1990–91	28.5	98.4	28.9

creating a layer of fertilized ash above the soil into which the seedlings were set. Planting did not consider soil erosion, and bushes grew in full sun, sucking out the ground's goodness. Production was augmented by bringing more virgin land into the system.

The large estates (*fazendas*) owned by the wealthy elite used slave labour. Each slave might tend 4,000–7,000 plants. Little maintenance was carried out. The natural drying process was used, prior to hulling and despatching to Rio on mule trains. Lack of soil maintenance contributed to the Rio beans' poor reputation, being prone to mould and off-flavours. Today, 'Rio-y' still describes such defects.

After the U.S. banned imports of slaves in 1807, North American slave traders shifted to the Brazilian market, setting up a triangular exchange: American goods traded into Africa, in exchange for slaves who were sold in Brazil, to buy coffee for delivery back to the U.S. This lasted until 1850 when the British ended the Atlantic slave trade through direct naval intervention.

Existing slaves (around one-third of the population) remained central to the Brazilian economy. An internal slave

Watercolour of slaves carrying coffee, based on Jean-Baptiste Debret, *A Voyage to Brazil*, 1834. The leader plays the thumb piano to set the pace.

market developed with southern Brazilian coffee planters buying slaves from the north. Only in 1871 was the so-called 'Law of the Free Womb' passed, making children of slaves free from birth, followed in 1888 by the 'Golden Law' freeing all remaining slaves.

In 1872 Brazil's imperial family was overthrown. A new republic was created, dominated by the *Paulistas*, the coffee barons of São Paulo state.

Dominance of São Paulo, City and State

The *Paulistas* replaced slave labour forces with poor European immigrants, known as *colonos*. They worked for wages on large coffee estates, but were given housing and a small plot to grow their own food. In 1884 the Brazilian state began subsidizing initial costs of transporting migrants, and by 1903 over

2 million had arrived. Over half came from Italy, attracted by the promise of land, but found they effectively became indentured labourers, required to pay back the cost of their voyage. The terms were so harsh that the Italian government banned subsidized migration schemes in 1902. Portugal and Spain then became principal sources of Brazilian *colonos*.

Coffee production rose phenomenally in this era – from 5.5 million sacks in 1890 to 16.3 million in 1901. Brazil accounted for 73 per cent of world coffee output between 1901 and 1905. Most was grown in the São Paulo region, where over 500 million coffee trees had been planted by 1900,

Port of Santos, Brazil, 1930s. Workers unload coffee sacks and drop them down into an underground chute system that conveys them directly into the hold of a ship.

An Italian coffee farm worker in Brazil in the 1930s.

meaning this one state alone produced nearly half of the coffee grown throughout the world.

The dramatic increase was achieved by bringing more and more land under cultivation. The coffee frontier spread south and west across São Paulo, moving through the central highlands into the state's hinterlands. Trading shifted to the port of Santos, assisted by São Paulo's extensive railroad development, including lines solely for transporting coffee.

The 1905 agricultural census captured the characteristics of the São Paulo coffee economy. Sixty-five per cent of the workforce on the 21,000 coffee farms in the state was foreign-born. The top 20 per cent of farmers controlled 83 per cent of the land, produced 75 per cent of the coffee and employed 67 per cent of the agricultural labour force. The biggest producer, the German-born Francesco Schmidt, owned 7 million coffee trees and employed over 4,000 workers.

The *Paulistas'* agriculture system did not create a coffee monoculture, however. It was common for *colonos* to grow food crops among coffee trees, and many *fazendas* practised mixed farming. The state of São Paulo was self-sufficient in food.[11]

Valorization

Brazil's world coffee market dominance reached its zenith in 1906, when it produced 20.2 million bags of coffee, around 85 per cent of the total world output. This bumper crop forced a change in the country's coffee strategy. During the nineteenth century Brazil had increased its coffee revenues by expanding production while maintaining low wholesale prices that stimulated demand. At the turn of the century, however, supply overtook demand, and prices plummeted from 13 to 6 U.S. cents per pound.

In 1906 the São Paulo state government subsidized a consortium of bankers and brokers led by Hermann Sielcken, a German-American coffee merchant, to buy up the coffee surplus and keep it off the market. By 1910 prices recovered to over 10 cents per pound and most of the syndicate's holdings were sold off by the end of 1913.

This 'valorization' of the coffee price orchestrated by Brazilian authorities was a significant moment in coffee's history: it was the first time producer countries had dictated trade terms to consumer nations. It caused outrage in the U.S., where Sielcken was hauled before a congressional committee in 1912. His explanation that there would have been a revolution in São Paulo without this scheme met with an unsympathetic response: 'Do you think that would have been a worse condition than that we [U.S.] should pay 14 cents a pound?'[12]

Valorization was regularly used by Brazilian authorities to regulate the amount of coffee on the world market thereafter, maintaining export prices at over 20 cents per pound. The São Paulo state started an agency to organize coffee interests, which was subsequently transformed into the national Instituto Brasileiro do Café (IBC).

The 1930s Great Depression destroyed this progress. The problem was a massive supply increase caused by new land being brought into production, with bumper crops being recorded every other year from 1927 onwards. The Brazilian harvest alone exceeded world demand in these years. By 1930 Brazil held 26 million bags in reserve stocks. Prices crashed to under 10 cents for the rest of the decade.

The IBC managed what became a desperate response by the authorities. Between 1931 and 1939 a network of 75 huge

The boiler of a train engine being fed a mixture of coffee and tar, as part of efforts to reduce the coffee surplus, Brazil, 1932.

incineration plants was established and 80 million bags of coffee (three years' global supply) went up in smoke. Tax penalties on new plantings were introduced and alternative uses for coffee were found, including making coffee bricks to fuel trains. The IBC tried to promote consumption through advertising and by opening Brazilian coffee houses in Europe, Russia and Japan.

Central America

Another cause of Brazil's problems was that its dominance of world supply had diminished with the emergence of Colombia and the Central America states – Costa Rica, El Salvador, Guatemala, Honduras, Nicaragua and Panama, plus Mexico. Until 1914 Brazil provided 75 per cent of U.S. coffee imports; between the First and Second World Wars, this fell to around 50 per cent. Furthermore, coffees from these other states enjoyed a significant price premium on the U.S. exchanges.

That premium derived from their coffees' superior cup quality, a reflection of the greater care in cultivation and harvesting, and using wet processing. This was undertaken at washing stations, or *beneficios*, which became the central point in connecting cultivators to the market. Large estates often operated their own processing plants, but small producers usually sold their cherries directly to the *beneficio*. *Beneficios* often extended credit to planters, effectively tying them into supplier deals. This placed *beneficio* operators in a strong position to ensure they received good-quality, ripe cherries, requiring selective picking throughout the season.

Central American states needed export earnings and encouraged their coffee frontiers into remote uncultivated, though often populated, highland regions. Conversion to

The traditional painted oxcarts or *carreta*, here in Costa Rica, were originally used by growers to carry coffee on a fifteen-day journey from the highlands of the central valley to the port of Puntarenas on the Pacific coast, from where it was shipped to San Francisco. In 2008 the *carreta* was inscribed into the UNESCO Representative List of the Intangible Cultural Heritage of Humanity.

commercial coffee growing required parcelling up land into private holdings, and creating a workforce with a sufficient stake to produce coffee to the quality levels required. Much of the year-round cultivation was undertaken by peasants working small-scale, often household-production units, whether as independent owners or within a variety of tenancy agreements.[13] This still left the issue of where to recruit pickers, however.

A range of solutions emerged according to circumstance. In El Salvador, vagrancy laws were used to force native populations from their lands and turn them into labourers on plantation-style estates. This generated a class of coffee oligarchs, effectively controlling the country, creating inequalities and conflicts that persisted throughout the twentieth century. In 1932 a revolt of impoverished coffee workers resulted in the *Matanza* (massacre) of tens of thousands of indigenous Salvadorans by government forces.

Conversely, in Costa Rica, the government passed homesteading laws, allowing settlers to claim titles to unoccupied land on the high plateaus where few native inhabitants were to be found. These settlers established independent smallholdings with backing from the *beneficios*, who in turn operated on credit supplied by importing firms mainly based in London, which functioned as an entrepôt for Costa Rican coffee.

Guatemala became the first Central American state to make a significant impression in the global market, becoming the world's fourth-largest coffee exporter by the end of the nineteenth century. Under the Liberal Premier General Barrios, in the 1870s, foreign purchasers could acquire large estates, tempted in by adverts in European papers such as *Le Monde*. Coffee growers exploited laws allowing departmental governors to compel villages to supply labourers, securing themselves seasonal workers for harvesting. German nationals were attracted into the country, and by the early twentieth century owned 10 per cent of the coffee farms (*fincas*), processed 40 per cent of the coffee harvest and controlled 80 per cent of the country's exports.

The outbreak of the First World War severely disrupted the European coffee market. This intensified a reorientation of Central American exports towards the United States, which began when San Francisco broker Clarence Bickford started sample cuppings with his buyers in the 1900s. These demonstrated that classifying beans by their colour and size alone (as done on the New York exchange) was inadequate for determining quality. Small-sized beans such as Guatemala's had been traded at a discount – now they enjoyed a premium.[14]

San Francisco's port and improved rail links made it a distribution hub for Central American coffee throughout the U.S. The opening of the Panama Canal in 1914 facilitated connections between coffee-exporting Pacific seaports of Central and Latin America and receiving ports in the North American and European markets. In 1913 U.S. imports of coffee from Central America totalled 36.3 million pounds; in 1918 they reached 195.3 million.

Colombia

After the First World War, Colombia emerged as the world's second-largest coffee producer – increasing output from 61,000 metric tons in 1913 to 101,000 in 1919 and 256,000 in 1938.

Coffee was supposedly introduced to Colombia by Jesuit priests, some of whom required their parishioners to plant coffee trees as an act of penance. Production was established on the mountainsides of the Andes' three branches (*cordilleras*), from north to south. Difficult terrain made railroad construction uneconomical, so coffee was brought by mule train to the Magdalena and Cauca rivers for shipment to the Caribbean ports of Barranquilla and Cartagena, or conveyed using an aerial cable car-style system to Buenaventura on the Pacific coast.

Commercial cultivation expanded in the late nineteenth century. Bogotá and Medellín merchants invested in coffee *haciendas* in the three departments of Santander, Cundinamarca and Antioquia. Inspired by Guatemala's success, they introduced similar techniques of planting shade plants to avoid soil erosion, selective picking of ripe cherries and wet processing. They relied principally on family units for production under different tenure systems – sharecropping in Santander, tenant farming in Antioquia and extensive estates known as *latifundia* in Cundinamarca.

During the 1920s Colombia's coffee output doubled, responding to the high prices obtained via the Brazilian valorization schemes and Colombia's quality premium of over 20 per cent. The coffee frontier moved south into Caldas, Tolima and Huila. Coffee accounted for 60–80 per cent of the country's exports, but left the Colombian industry highly exposed to the Brazilian bumper harvests and subsequent price collapse during the Great Depression. Social conflict ensued as landowners attempted to pass on their losses by altering contract terms with cultivators. Many disputes descended into violence, notably on the *latifundia*.

At this juncture, the Colombian state stepped in, founding the Federación Nacional de Caféteros de Colombia (National Federation of Colombian Coffee Growers) in 1927 to act as 'a private entity carrying out essential public functions for the

Colombia, 1970s–80s. Hand-picking on the mountain slopes. As this image shows, mechanization is not an option for Colombian coffee growers.

national interest'.[15] Funded by the introduction of a levy on every bag of coffee leaving the country, its remit was to manage the country's coffee policy in the 'best interests' of its growers. As well as providing educational, financial and technical services to its members, the FNCC regulates the country's exports sector and promotes Colombian coffee abroad.

Its wide-ranging powers enabled the FNCC to effectively manipulate the price premium between Colombian and Brazilian coffee. During the 1930s it deliberately lowered the differential to obtain greater market share in the United States. By 1937 Colombia had captured 25 per cent of the U.S. market.

Inter-American Coffee Agreement

The collapse of the coffee price during the Depression forced the leading Latin American producers to start negotiating with each other to find solutions to the crisis. In 1936 they established the Pan-American Coffee Bureau to promote consumption in the United States, while the Brazilian IBC and Colombian FNCC entered into a price maintenance agreement, which quickly fell apart, with Brazil accusing Colombia of 'free-riding' on Brazilian efforts to regulate the coffee supply by withholding stocks from the market. In 1938 Brazil flooded the market with coffee in frustration, driving prices back down, but following the outbreak of war in Europe in 1939, it became imperative for producers to find a way to avert any further price collapse.

On 28 November 1940, the Inter-American Coffee Agreement was signed by all fourteen coffee-producing states in the western hemisphere along with the United States, which recognized the value of ensuring the stability of supply. The agreement stated, 'It is necessary and desirable to take steps to promote the orderly marketing of coffee, with a view to assuring terms of trade equitable for both producers and consumers by adjusting supply to demand.'[16]

The national agencies representing the coffee producers negotiated quotas for their exports to the United States, with the system entering into force in April 1941. By the end of the year prices had doubled, and they remained strong thereafter.

Creating Consumers

Consumption levels in the United States rose steadily throughout the first half of the twentieth century. Average annual coffee imports into the U.S. doubled between 1915–20 and 1946–50. Even the Great Depression failed to halt this progress. By 1939 coffee had become an everyday household good – 98 per cent of U.S. households reported drinking it.

Coffee's fortunes were favoured by broader developments in American society. Prohibition between 1920 and 1933 saw cafés supplant saloons, so coffee rather than alcohol became the legally sanctioned beverage for socializing outside the home. An increasing emphasis on a light lunch during the working day resulted in more daytime consumption of coffee. Even so, the principal venue for coffee consumption was the home.

But What Did the Consumer Want?

A 1924 survey for J. Walter Thompson established that 87 per cent of housewives cited flavour as the most important factor in their choice of blend. However, 'it is extremely difficult for the average person to make clear distinctions where flavour is concerned'.[17]

The Texan retailer Harry Longe said the market was segmented into four types of purchasers – all housewives – and came up with 'Any Blend' messages to appeal to each of them.[18]

The 'Know-it-all-about-Coffee' who cannot find anything to suit her cultivated taste:

IMPROVE THE COFFEE AND YOU IMPROVE THE MEAL

The corner of the table that holds the coffee pot is the balancing point of your dinner. If the coffee is a 'little off' for some reason or other – probably it's the coffee's own fault – things don't seem as good as they might; but when it is 'up to taste' the meal is a pleasure from start to finish. If the 'balancing point' is giving you trouble, let *ANY BLEND* coffee properly regulate it for you.

The bride of a few months who knows very little about coffee, but wants to find a good blend that she and her husband can rely on:

A SUCCESSFUL SELECTION

of the coffee that goes into the every-morning cup will arrive on the day when *ANY BLEND* is first purchased. Many homes have been without a success for a long time, but of course, they didn't know of *ANY BLEND* – and even now it is hard to really know *ANY BLEND* until you try it. That is why we seem to insist that you ask for an introduction by ordering a pound.

Those satisfied with their existing coffee:
A SERVICE THAT SAVES
is the serving of *ANY BLEND*, when coffee is desired. *ANY BLEND* saves many things. It saves worry, for it is always uniform in flavour and strength. It saves time, for when you order *ANY BLEND* we grind it just as fine or as coarse as your percolator or pot demands. *ANY BLEND* also saves expense, because there is no waste, as you know just how much to use, every time, to make a certain number of cups.

And for households with staff:
CAN YOU NAME YOUR COFFEE?
or is it one of those many unknown brands that comes from the store at the order of your cook? Let the cook do the ordering, for you are lucky if you have one you can rely upon, but tell her you prefer *ANY BLEND* to the No-Name blend you may now be using. *ANY BLEND* has one distinct advantage over all others; it is freshly roasted. Tell the kitchen-lady, now, to order *ANY BLEND*.

Longe's words played on consumers' lack of confidence about coffee. Coffee was regarded as representing the household to outsiders, so he created anxiety about its quality. Getting it right was presented as vital to domestic harmony – no new bride wants to live in a 'home without success'.

Brands and Advertising

By the end of the 1930s, over 90 per cent of roasted coffee was purchased in pre-weighed, trademarked packages. There were over 5,000 coffee brands, but the three leading players

– A&P, Maxwell House, and Chase & Sanborn – held 40 per cent of the market. Their dominance was partially due to over half of all purchases being made in grocery chain outlets, such as those operated by A&P. By 1929 Maxwell House and Chase & Sanborn had been acquired by General Foods and Standard Brands, respectively – two huge corporations who utilized their economic power to ensure the brands were given prominence on supermarket shelves.

Manufacturers began persuasive communications campaigns, utilizing the mass channels that developed in the interwar era. Advertising agencies produced campaigns like Maxwell House's advertisements in glossy magazines, featuring the original sophisticated hotel and President Teddy Roosevelt's alleged endorsement that the coffee was 'good to the last drop'. A sponsored radio variety programme – *The Maxwell House Show Boat* – was introduced in 1933, and soon became the country's top show. Hollywood celebrities sipped coffee while chatting to presenters between music and acts, while listeners were reminded that 'your ticket of admission is just your loyalty to Maxwell House coffee.' Within a year of the show's launch, sales had risen by 85 per cent.[19]

Much of the major roasters' messaging played on the sense of unease around coffee identified by Longe. Chase & Sanborn regularly ran advertisements where wives were reproached by their husbands for failing to serve satisfactory coffee. Such adverts were meant to be educational, urging readers to purchase 'dated' coffee (stamped with the day of store delivery) and vacuum packs, to ensure freshness. Even then, Hills Brothers, institutors of the process, disclaimed, 'The coffee is turned over to you in perfect condition. Here our responsibility ceases, and unless you will cooperate with us by seeing that the coffee is made properly, our efforts and your money will be wasted.'[20]

War and After

The U.S. entry into the Second World War saw a brief period of rationing between 1942 and 1943, but wartime experiences further increased coffee's popularity.

Soldiers proved avid consumers, encouraged by officers who realized the value for morale. As in the Civil War, coffee seems to have served as stimulant and comfort, and perhaps a relief from monotony. An early post-war study of the Navy suggested that, while at sea, sailors consumed twice as much as civilians – even onshore personnel drank 50 per cent more than the national average.[21]

Munitions workers proved more productive when allowed the new 'coffee breaks'. These were introduced throughout the military. The practice spread into post-war civilian life, with around 60 per cent of factories adopting it by the mid-1950s. This was partly a consequence of the Pan-American Coffee Bureau's heavy promotional campaign in favour of workplace coffee breaks. It also advocated 'coffee breaks on the road', arguing that coffee kept drivers alert in an increasingly motorized America.

A survey in winter 1954 found that consumers drank an average of two and a half cups a day. Two cups were drunk at home – usually at breakfast and dinner – with the remainder taken either in cafés/restaurants or at work. City dwellers enjoyed 2.8 cups per day, and those in rural districts averaged 2.3 cups. The highest levels of consumption, however, were found in the Midwestern farming belt, perhaps reflecting the Scandinavian origins of many of its inhabitants.

Immediately following the Second World War, U.S. consumption levels per capita reached an all-time peak of over 8.6 kilograms (19 lb) per person for those over ten years old. Latin America was producing 85 per cent of the world's output and sending 70 per cent of it to the U.S., where coffee was now consumed in virtually every household. The concept of the American 'cup of Joe' – a term for 'ordinary coffee' that first appeared in the 1930s – was firmly established. This presented as a thin-bodied, weak-flavoured coffee served in a comparatively large volume to accompany meals. Its taste profile reflected the blandness of the Brazilian beans at its base, the over-extracted coffee that resulted from brewing

A waitress pours coffee for a customer at a U.S. diner in 1941. The classic American 'cup of joe' was prepared using pour-over machines and left warming on the hotplate, to provide unlimited refills.

with a percolator, and the parsimoniousness of American housewives with the quantities of coffee they used.

By the end of the 1950s, however, it was already clear that consumption levels in the U.S. were declining as the younger generation turned to soft drinks, with Europe on the verge of overtaking North America as the leading consumer continent. Latin American producers, meanwhile, were again suffering low prices caused by oversupply, exacerbated by the rise of new players in Africa and Asia growing cheaper Robusta. Coffee had become a global commodity.

5
Global Commodity

Coffee became a global commodity during the second half of the twentieth century. The foundation was the planting of Robusta as a hardier alternative to Arabica, reviving coffee production in Africa and Asia. Its cheaper price facilitated everyday coffee drinking among new consumers, and dramatically altered the beverage's taste and forms. International institutions developed to regulate the world coffee market, but proved incapable of protecting producers from price volatility, culminating in the coffee crisis at the century's end.

Robusta and the African Revival

Robusta varieties from the Belgian Congo were introduced into the Dutch East Indies during the 1900s to replace Arabica plants lost to coffee rust. By the 1930s over 90 per cent of the East Indies output was Robusta. This found a ready market among American roasters, enabling them to advertise that their blends contained Java or Sumatra. The Second World War and subsequent Independence wars destroyed much Indonesian coffee production. It was not until the 1980s that Indonesia again became the world's largest Robusta producer.

Leading Producer States by Decade[1]

1960s	1970s	1980s	1990s	2000s	2010s
Brazil	Brazil	Brazil	Brazil	Brazil	Brazil
Colombia	Colombia	Colombia	Colombia	Vietnam	Vietnam
Angola	Ivory Coast	Indonesia	Indonesia	Colombia	Colombia
Uganda	Mexico	Mexico	Vietnam	Ethiopia	Indonesia
Ivory Coast	Indonesia	Ivory Coast	Guatemala	India	Ethiopia
Mexico	Ethiopia	Ethiopia	India	Mexico	India

Robusta returned Africa to a central role within the global coffee economy that it had not known since the decline of Mocha. By 1965 the continent accounted for 23 per cent of world production compared to 2 per cent in 1914.[2] Seventy-five per cent of this output was Robusta, principally grown in the former French and Belgian colonies of West and Central Africa, as well as Uganda and Angola.

Robusta coffee plants in Sumatra, 1924, planted in the shade of rubber trees on a Dutch-owned plantation.

Drying coffee cherries for natural processing, Ivory Coast.

The Ivory Coast raised production from under 16,000 tonnes in 1939 to 114,000 tonnes in 1958. Production expanded rapidly after independence in 1960, reaching 279,500 tonnes in 1970. Levels maintained over the next twenty years. During the 1970s, the Ivory Coast was the third-largest coffee producer in the world (after Brazil and Colombia), and the leading Robusta exporter. Credit is due to Félix Houphouët-Boigny, the country's first president.

Houphouët-Boigny was a coffee farmer who campaigned against the French plantation owners' privileges in the colonial era, particularly their exploitation of involuntary labour. Once these advantages were removed, native growers proved more efficient. After independence, Houphouët-Boigny urged his compatriots not to 'vegetate in bamboo huts' but to concentrate on growing good coffee to 'become rich'.[3] He retained the French *Caisse de stabilisation* – the 'stabilization fund' agency. This set prices for buying and selling coffee at all stages. It connected producers to processors and exporters. Although trade remained in private hands, the government protected growers by offering guaranteed prices, thereby encouraging new land into production in the country's central forest zones.

The *Caisse* system was used by nearly all the Francophone African states. It was financed through a tax applied on exporters' profits. The aim was to accumulate revenues during high world prices to maintain the returns to producers when prices were low, and to invest in raising productivity and agricultural diversification. This worked comparatively well in the Ivory Coast. Farmers received an average of 70 per cent of the world price between 1974 and 1982. The temptation to drive down the internal prices paid to producers to generate surpluses to support non-economic government projects proved too much for many states, however, and the *Caisse* frequently became a font of institutional corruption.

States formerly under British rule maintained the marketing boards introduced by colonial authorities. These purchased processed beans for export, and returned the exchange received to the state. The marketing boards undertook sorting, grading and blending. They rewarded quality production through the differential prices they paid for coffee that could be included in premium lots.

In Kenya, white settlers, most famously Karen Blixen, set up farms in the early twentieth century. They planted Arabica, but used Bourbon varieties rather than the Typica that originated in Ethiopia. This partly explains the contrast between the floral, citrus-like flavours found in Ethiopian coffees, and the jammy, blackberry taste of many Kenyan origins. In the 1950s, following the Mau Mau uprising, agricultural reforms were introduced that encouraged the establishment of family holdings combining subsistence farming with the planting of cash crops, notably coffee. After independence in 1963, the Kenyan government retained the Coffee Board's central auction system, whereby exporters purchased lots classified

Grading green coffee samples in Kenya, *c.* 1980s. Strict quality controls secured coffee's role as a key source of foreign exchange earnings following independence in 1963. Only since 2002 have Kenyans been able to buy and consume coffee grown and roasted in their own country.

according to cup characteristics, and growers received the average price for their class, thereby rewarding quality. By contrast, in newly independent Tanzania, coffee was sold by the Coffee Board in homogeneous lots, and quickly lost its reputation, which only began to be restored following reforms in the mid-1990s.

Uganda meanwhile became a leading volume producer of Robusta, increasing production from 31,000 tonnes in the late 1940s to 119,000 by independence in 1962. In 1969 this peaked at 247,000 tonnes, most of which was grown by smallholders on garden plots in areas like the Lake Victoria Crescent.

Unusually, the Ugandan producers washed their Robusta, raising its quality. Production began to fall from the mid-1970s because of the Amin dictatorship's disastrous policies and the subsequent decade of political and military instability. The Coffee Marketing Board grew into a bloated bureaucracy, returning less than 20 per cent of their coffee's market price to the farmers, despite coffee being responsible for over 90 per cent of the country's export earnings.[4]

Instant Coffee

In 1929 the Brazilian authorities, desperate for alternative uses for their surplus beans, approached the Swiss multinational food manufacturer Nestlé to ask if it could develop a coffee stock cube. It took Nestlé research scientist Max Morgenthaler over six years to come up with a palatable soluble coffee, by which time both Brazilian interest, and his own research team, had long been withdrawn.[5]

Nescafé, a spray-dried extract, was launched in 1938. War in Europe led to concentration of production in the U.S., where the War Department bought up virtually all production for military use. It returned to Europe in GIs' backpacks and the CARE (Cooperative for American Remittances to Europe) packages despatched at the war's end. In 1965 freeze-dried Nescafé Gold Blend was launched as a premium product, packaged in jars.

The major American roasters also started producing soluble coffees. Maxwell House's version overtook Nescafé in the U.S. in 1953. By the end of the decade solubles had a 20 per cent market share, primarily at the low-price end of the grocery sector. They, like Nescafé, used blends composed of upwards of 50 per cent Robusta beans.

'Ah – just like freshly roasted whole bean coffee'. A Nescafé advertisement – one of the earliest examples of packaging in glass jars.

Instant coffee came to define national taste preferences and consumption practices within underdeveloped markets. In the tea-dominated UK, coffee consumption doubled during the 1950s, coinciding with the launch of commercial television. Viewers found advertising breaks gave them sufficient time to make a cup of instant coffee, but not to brew a traditional cup of tea. By the 1990s coffee was outselling tea in terms of value (not volume), with instant coffee comprising 90 per cent of sales. Nescafé's iconic 'Gold Blend Couple' TV campaign, launched in 1987 – featuring a will-they-won't-they relationship between two neighbours – entrenched its position as the market leader. Over half the UK population tuned in to watch the final episode in December 1992, and the campaign is claimed to have increased sales by 70 per cent.[6]

At a trade fair in Thessaloniki, Greece, in 1957, a Nescafé representative mixed instant powder and cold water in a cocoa drink shaker, creating a thick foam. Diluted with more water and served over ice, it proved very refreshing. The company began promoting this new use, which was adopted by young Greeks, becoming a symbol of the outdoor lifestyle. Frappé became Greece's national summer beverage.[7]

Emergence of European Coffee Styles

The advent of Robusta significantly changed the profiles of other national tastes in post-war Europe. By 1960, 75 per cent of coffee consumed in France was Robusta, necessitating the use of dark caramelized roasts to counteract the beans' bitterness. The most popular Dutch and Belgian roasts were also medium-dark, reflecting their ties to Robusta-producing former colonies. Italy developed regional preferences,with an increasing emphasis on Robusta the further south one travelled. While this initially reflected the coffee's cheapness, it became an enshrined consumer preference. Portugal developed its own espresso-style beverage – the *bica* – brewed with blends of Robusta from Angola, where production, principally from white-owned estates, reached 225,000 tonnes in the early 1970s until the outbreak of the independence wars disrupted the industry.

The coffee industry's evolution in Europe during the twentieth century led to distinctive 'national tastes', with markets adopting different forms of brewing technology, roasts, blends and consumption habits. Many 'traditional' coffee styles we associate with particular countries date back no further than the last century. Often these were only consolidated in the mass consumer societies that arose after the Second World War. Local and regional roasters lost out as small grocers and specialist coffee shops declined, and supermarkets took over. These stocked the highly visible branded products that shoppers recognized from expensive television advertising campaigns on behalf of dominant 'national' roasters. Consumed in a similar fashion across classes, drinking coffee became an everyday expression of 'national identity'.

Germany

Germany became Europe's largest coffee market following its 1871 unification. By the 1900s coffee was drunk daily across all regions and classes, providing families with a warm accompaniment to morning and evening meals of bread or potatoes. Surrogate products satisfied a significant portion of this demand: in 1914, 160 million kilograms (350 million lb) of coffee substitutes were consumed along with 180 million kilograms (400 million lb) of coffee.[8]

Consumption rituals developed, such as the *Kaffeeklatsch* – women gathering for an afternoon chat with coffee and cake. Coffee stalls flourished in large cities, serving workers going to, or on a break from, the factory or office. At Sunday family gatherings, the 'best' coffee – made with real beans, not ersatz substitutes – would be produced, while summer afternoons might culminate with a stroll to the local park's coffee gardens. In some of these, hot water was sold, allowing less well-off patrons to brew up coffee they had brought with them.

Hamburg became Europe's leading coffee port, with around 90 per cent of imports now coming from Latin America, many shipped through the networks established by German émigré enterprises.[9] The coffee exchange, founded in 1887, counted some two hundred member organizations of importers, brokers and merchants by the start of the twentieth century. Consignments were graded and sorted by women warehouse workers, with despatch samples placed in special coffee 'postboxes' in the port. Rail networks carried the coffee to the numerous wholesalers and grocers around the country.

In the 1880s van Guelpen, Lensing and von Gimborn, the Rhineland-based engineering firm that later became Probat, started producing drum roasters. These were used to set up wholesale coffee-roasting businesses supplying predominantly loose beans to local grocery stores. It was only later that roasters established their own branded identities, mostly confined to regional markets.

The major exceptions were brands linked to larger direct distribution operations, such as Kaiser's Kaffee, the own-brand food store chain, which had 1,420 stores on the eve of the First World War. Eduscho, the Bremen-based mail-order house, became the largest roaster in Germany during the 1930s.

Tasters checking roasted samples for Jacobs, one of the world's largest roasters, West Germany, 1980s.

In the immediate post-war era Tchibo, founded in Hamburg as a mail-order operator in 1949, transformed itself into West Germany's leading roaster, with a chain of small outlets during the 1950s and '60s. Here coffee could be sampled in-store and beans purchased for home. In the 1970s Tchibo extended into in-store operations within bakeries and supermarkets. In 1997 Tchibo and Eduscho merged into one company.

The German preference was increasingly for filter coffee. In 1908 Dresden housewife Melitta Bentz patented a new preparation system using paper filters, set into a brass filter pot with punched holes. Supposedly she developed this by experimenting with her son's school blotting paper. Previous filter systems had relied on using cloths that were washed and re-used. Now housewives could clear up by throwing out the filter paper and grounds. Her husband established the company bearing her name, which was immediately successful, cementing its hold in the 1930s when the now-familiar cone-shaped filters and papers were introduced.

Scandinavia

The Nordic countries also developed a strong regional coffee culture. This arose from the combination of coffee's functional benefits as a warming beverage against the cold, and the temperance movement, closely linked to the church, which promoted coffee as an alternative to alcohol. Coffee consumption per capita in Denmark and Sweden already exceeded the United States in the 1930s. By the 1950s Finland had the highest coffee consumption per capita in the world, closely followed by Norway.

Sami reindeer herders routinely drank twelve cups of coffee a day in the 1950s. The men warmed themselves with coffee before leaving in the morning. When the women heard the dogs barking announcing their return, they prepared fresh coffee. Coffee drinking was central to their hospitality ritual. This demanded visitors be offered, and accept, a minimum of two cups of coffee per visit, which could push up daily consumption to twenty cups.[10]

Urban communities also developed routines and rituals organized around coffee. *Fika* – a time to share coffee and cake with family, friends or one's work colleagues – evolved in Sweden during the late nineteenth century. Its centrality in the country's culture is such that today refugees are inducted into the practice. The Danish language acquired specific

The ‘real’ Paula Girl has served refreshing coffee from her copper pan for more than fifty years. The third Paula, Anja Mustamäki, held the post from 1962 to 1969.

terms to describe the coffee prepared for a woman giving birth and the attendant midwife. Finnish labour legislation officially established coffee breaks during the working day.[11]

The Scandinavian preference is for light-roasted coffee. Industrial roasters perpetuate this style to reflect national distinctiveness. Paulig, the major Finnish roaster, placed an image of a young woman in national costume pouring coffee from a kettle on its branded products in the 1920s. Since the 1950s, Paulig has selected a young woman to be the Paula girl, who promotes the brand through public appearances.

Italy

Italy evolved a distinctive European coffee culture, due to its development of espresso brewing.[12] The spread of upmarket cocktail bars where drinks were quickly prepared and passed to customers across the counter led to a demand from the hospitality industry for equally swift ways of serving coffee. Applying pressure to the brewing process speeded up the extraction time, enabling a fresh cup of coffee to be prepared 'expressly' for each customer. The first commercially produced machine was the La Pavoni Ideale manufactured in Milan in 1905. It incorporated a boiler from which steam was drawn to drive hot water down through the coffee clamped onto a delivery outlet ('group head'). As the pressures were relatively low (1.5 to 2 bar), the preparation process still took around a minute, and produced a concentrated filter-coffee taste. These large, highly decorative machines sat on the bar counters of many top European hotels. The Fascist regime's suspicion of coffee as a 'foreign luxury' meant ordinary Italians were more familiar with coffee substitutes.

This changed after 1948 when Achille Gaggia produced a new espresso machine that utilized a lever connected to a spring-loaded piston to blast water through the coffee. It achieved higher pressures (around 9 bars), the delivery speed was much quicker (around 25 seconds) and the resultant extract was topped with a mousse or *crema* of essential oils. Subsequently manufacturers, notably Faema, introduced semi-automatic machines, replacing the piston with an electric pump. A coffee from the bar now looked, and tasted, different from anything prepared at home. The same was true for cappuccino – originally meaning coffee with milk, but now used exclusively for espresso with steamed milk, and only available at the bar.

The 1950s and '60s saw the emergence of modern Italian coffee culture. Industrialization and urbanization led to an increase of neighbourhood coffee bars serving the small workshops and housing estates generated by migration from countryside to city. The speed of coffee preparation and drinking made bars ideal places for grabbing a cappuccino before work and for quick breaks during the day. Drinking coffee on one's feet became standard, not least because of a 1911 law allowing councils to impose a maximum price for 'a cup of coffee without service' – that is, standing at the counter. Set low to curb inflation, this made the coffee bar sector unattractive to corporate chains.

A key advantage of the espresso process is that it intensifies flavours so cheaper commodity beans can form significant portions of the blend. In the post-war era Brazil sold off stocks of low-grade Santos to Italy, where roasters also turned to Robusta, which had the added advantage of producing a thicker, visually appealing *crema*.

Domestic consumption doubled between 1955 and 1970. The aluminium, eight-sided stovetop brewer known as the 'Moka Express', manufactured by Bialetti, became standard equipment in Italian kitchens. It functions as a percolator: water heated in the lower chamber is forced up through the coffee by steam pressure to collect in the serving section at the top. It was advertised as producing coffee 'just like that at the bar', even though no *crema* is created.

In the 1960s the Lavazza company from Piedmont became the first coffee producer with a nationwide presence. Its success was due to an innovative television-advertising campaign using animated cartoon characters, combined with an extensive distribution system that penetrated the many neighbourhood stores throughout the country. In 1995, a hundred years after Luigi Lavazza opened a grocery roasting

Rome, Italy, 1957. The barman is using a Gaggia machine, the first to use high pressures resulting in a head of essential oils on the espresso. This was dubbed *crema caffè*, as seen in the slogan on the front of the machine.

coffee in Turin, the company had a 45 per cent share of the 'at-home' Italian market.

Central Europe

The Viennese coffee house reached the peak of its fame in the early twentieth century. This success coincided with the democratization of culture and consumption that characterized the European *fin de siècle*. By 1902 there were around 1,100 cafés in the city, appealing to a broad middle-class clientele, along with over 4,000 working-class taverns.[13]

The public accessibility of the coffee houses was a key part of their appeal to groups such as Vienna's Jewish population who still encountered prejudice within Austrian society. The Young Vienna literary circle, containing many Jewish writers, met at the Café Griensteidl. Socialist thinkers including

Leon Trotsky frequented the Café Central. These groups would occupy a *Stammtisch*, a table reserved for regulars who would drop in over the course of the day. The largely male waiting staff, presided over by a major domo known as *Herr Ober*, meant there was little likelihood of coffee houses being mistaken for houses of ill repute. Female guests were welcome, but dark interiors and the masculine atmosphere meant many women preferred to meet each other for coffee at the cake shop or *Café-Konditorei.*

The coffee house phenomenon extended throughout the Austro-Hungarian Empire. In Budapest, there were around five hundred coffee houses operating in the early 1930s, the most beautiful surely was the New York, established in 1894. Trieste, the empire's outlet on the Adriatic, became one of Europe's leading coffee ports, a status it maintained after being transferred to Italy after the First World War. This was

Budapest, Hungary, 2006. Interior of the restored New York coffee house, originally opened in 1894.

how Ferenc Illy, born into a Hungarian family in what is now Timişoara in Romania, came to found one of Italy's leading coffee-roasting companies in 1933, having stayed in Trieste after serving in the Austro-Hungarian army during the war.

Julius Meinl, the proprietor of a Viennese colonial goods shop established in 1862, set up a roasting company that developed into Central Europe's largest coffee supplier under the leadership of his son Julius Meinl II. By 1928 it was operating 353 grocery stores in Austria, Hungary, Czechoslovakia, Yugoslavia, Poland and Romania. In 1938 Julius Meinl III, a prominent anti-Nazi married to a Jew, moved the family to London, returning after the war to rebuild the company's fortunes.

The Austrian coffee house developed an extensive menu of coffee beverages. In addition to the black, the brown, the gold and the *melange* (mixture), whose names capture the relative proportions of milk and coffee, more esoteric offerings included the one-horse carriage (a large amount of whipped cream on top of a black coffee in a glass) and the Sperber-Turk – a double-sized Turkish coffee boiled with a cube of sugar, first consumed by a famous lawyer.[14] From the 1950s, however, espresso machines were swiftly adopted in Viennese coffee houses, so that the *melange* and the cappuccino became very similar.

Elsewhere in Central Europe, coffee culture had to coexist with communism, and vice versa. The 'Standard Coffee Blend' made available in countries such as Czechoslovakia was often of dubious origin and content: in 1977 East Germany reacted to a currency crisis by launching Kaffee-MIX – ground coffee combined with roasted peas, rye, barley and sugar beet. In Hungary, neighbourhood *eszpresso* bars were concessions to the ingrained coffee culture, but it was only after 1989 that the New York and other Budapest coffee houses were restored to their original splendour. Coffee consumption in East and Central Europe has risen dramatically since the fall of the Berlin wall.

Japan

During the latter twentieth century, consumer markets outside Europe and North America assumed a significance within the global coffee trade. Mostly fuelled by convenience products, this resulted in the opening of long-established elite coffee cultures to the broader population.

Japan, today the world's third-largest importing country, exemplifies this. Coffee was first introduced to Japan by the Dutch East India Company in the late seventeenth century. It was confined to Dejima, the artificial island off Nagasaki, through which foreign trade was conducted during the Tokugawa shogunate, which maintained Japan as a 'closed country'. The only Japanese with a taste for coffee during this period were the island prostitutes who prized it for keeping them awake in order to prevent their clients from departing without paying.[15]

Coffee entered Japanese society in the later nineteenth century, after the Meiji restoration and American pressure to open the country for international trade. In 1888 Tei Ei-kei established the Kahiichakan, a coffee house modelled on those he experienced in New York and London. It was modelled on elite clubs: leather armchairs, carpets, newspapers, billiard tables and well-stocked writing desks. Sadly, selling access to all this for a single cup of coffee was not a viable business. Tei Ei-kei went bankrupt, dying in penury.

More commercial propositions were developed. The Café Paulista, a chain of *kissaten* (coffee shops with waiter service), were opened in the 1900s by Mizuno Ryu, who had been employed by Brazilian coffee plantations as part of a sponsorship programme to bring in Japanese workers as *colonos* after the Italian schemes ended. Japanese émigrés also worked on Hawaiian coffee farms during this era. As in Europe, the development of mass coffee culture in Japan was held back by the emphasis on autarchy in the interwar era.

Coffee import restrictions were only lifted in 1960. Japan imported 250,000 bags the following year. By 1990 the figure was 5.33 million bags. *Kissaten* started to spread through Japanese society from the mid-1960s. Proprietors were attracted because of relatively low entry costs, while customer numbers were fuelled by the country's economic boom. By 1970 there were 50,000 *kissaten*, peaking at 160,000 in 1982. Thereafter a division developed between older-style *kissaten* and Western-style, self-service café formats appealing to younger consumers. These included the Doutor coffee chain, which opened its first branch in 1980 and today has over nine hundred outlets.

Many *kissaten* developed their own preparation techniques and rituals, using special net filters or syphon equipment (originally introduced by the Dutch). This created opportunities for companies like Hario, a glassware maker, to produce high-specification, heat-retaining brewing equipment. The beans' origins also came to be appreciated, with Tanzanian Kilimanjaro gaining popularity due to the mountain's resemblance to the sacred Mount Fuji.

Mass-market development was driven by new convenience formats, notably ready-to-drink (RTD) beverages in cans. These were first produced by the Ueshima Coffee Company, which launched 'UCC Coffee with Milk' in 1969. The introduction of vending machines serving these hot and cold in 1973 created a substantial on-the-go 'industrial' coffee market. It is indicative of the popularity of sweetened beverages that it was

Ready-to-drink canned coffee drinks for sale in Japan.

nearly twenty years before UCC added a black sugarless coffee to its range.

Nonetheless it was soluble coffee that sparked the 'at-home' market growth, accounting for five out of 8.5 cups consumed weekly in 1983, enabling Nescafé to become a market leader.[16]

International Coffee Agreement

The politics of the global coffee trade reflected shifts in economic power within both the consumer and the producer segments. The emergence of large-scale national roasters exercising significant buying power was intensified when American grocery multinationals began buying brands to access overseas markets. In the 1970s General Foods acquired the Swedish roaster Gevalia and Sara Lee bought Douwe Egberts, based in the Netherlands. Phillip Morris added Jacobs Suchard to its roster in 1990. Nestlé, meanwhile, reversed the trend by acquiring U.S. brands such as Hills Brothers and Chase & Sanborne in the 1980s.

The rise in Robusta production fundamentally altered the supply side of the international coffee market. Prices fell after 1954 due to the world supply increasing, leading the Latin American producers to start limiting their exports in 1957. Their intervention failed because, as Robusta was priced lower than Arabica, new producers were unconcerned by Brazilian threats to dump coffee on the market. Withholding supplies simply incentivized buyers to switch to Robusta, leaving Brazil holding stocks equivalent to annual world consumption by 1959.

The Latin American countries began lobbying the United States for a global agreement introducing controls on imports as well as exports. They exploited political fears raised by the 1959 Cuban Revolution, with a Colombian senator urging, 'Pay us good prices for our coffee or – God help us all – the masses will become one great Marxist revolutionary army that will sweep us all into the sea.'[17] Given their reliance on Brazil and Colombia, the major U.S. roasters found it prudent to support an agreement while the Cuban Missile Crisis convinced Congress to ratify it. European consumer countries adhered so that their remaining colonies and newly independent producer states could achieve economic security.

The 1962 International Coffee Agreement (ICA) was signed by 44 exporting members and 26 importing ones. Its stated aim was:

> to achieve a reasonable balance between supply and demand on a basis which will assure adequate supplies of coffee to consumers and markets for coffee to producers at equitable prices and which will bring about long-term equilibrium between production and consumption.[18]

The agreement then established the International Coffee Organization (ICO), headquartered in London.

The ICO Council formed the supreme body for implementation. Proposals had to gain 70 per cent of the votes from producer and consumer members. Votes were assigned in proportion to the volume of members' exports or imports. Brazil held 346 of the 1,000 producer votes, and the USA four hundred of the 1,000 consumer ones. Target price bands for four forms of coffee were established: Colombian Milds, Other Milds, Brazilian Naturals and Robusta. Members were assigned quotas for each export type. When prices rose above the band, as they did following the devastating Brazilian frost of 1975, export quotas were relaxed to bring them down; if they fell below the band, they were tightened to raise it back up. The quota regime remained in operation from 1962 to 1989.

The balance of power in the global coffee chain shifted towards producer states, more specifically the quasi-state agencies representing them in the ICO. When consumer members were reluctant to enforce quotas in the early 1970s following the collapse of the Bretton Woods exchange rate system and the oil price shock, the largest producer agencies such as the IBC, FNCC and Ivorian *Caisse* collaborated by establishing joint entities to buy and sell coffee on the world markets. Using their specialist 'insider' knowledge of stocks and harvest forecasts, they successfully frustrated financial speculators efforts to manipulate futures prices.

The quota system remained in place throughout the 1980s, primarily for political reasons. Following Nicaragua's 1979 Sandinista revolution, the U.S. Reagan administration wanted to avoid further left-wing triumphs in the civil wars in El Salvador, Guatemala, Nicaragua and Colombia. These partially derived from the wealth distribution iniquities created

Frost-damaged coffee plants in Brazil. The 1975 'black frost' destroyed more than half a million trees in Brazil. Output fell by 60 per cent the following year, and the price of green coffee trebled between 1975 and 1977.

within their coffee-growing sectors. In Guatemala, 1 per cent of the coffee farms produced 56 per cent of the crop.[19] As in El Salvador, the indigenous peasantry who worked the farms became the targets of violent ethnic repression by military rulers. Conversely, guerrillas demanded 'war taxes' from middle-class farm owners, on pain of their buildings being burnt down and lands occupied. Under Sandinista rule, ENCAFE, the Nicaraguan coffee agency, returned only 10 per cent of the coffee export price to producers.[20]

The relatively secure returns delivered by the quota system compared to other commodities encouraged producers like the Philippines and Indonesia to increase their coffee output. An additional incentive was that the ICA established quotas balancing a 'demonstrated capacity' for production against 'historic' world-market share.

Most new production was Robusta, which was in demand for instant coffee products. Keen to exploit these new cheap supplies of coffee, importers developed 'coffee-cleaning' techniques, steaming the beans to moderate their bitterness. By 1976 Nestlé had established processing subsidiaries in 21 producer countries.[21] Some states set up their own enterprises: Ecuador planted and processed Robusta for export as coffee powder. Brazil introduced Conilon, a Robusta variety, in the state of Espirito Santo and developed a processing infrastructure. Soluble coffee has gained popularity among Brazilians, and today around 20 per cent of all Brazilian production is Robusta.

Some Central American state agencies took advantage of the stability to invest heavily into agricultural research to improve yields. So-called 'technification', including the introduction of dwarf cultivars capable of growing in full sun, and the use of chemical fertilizers, resulted in producers dramatically increasing outputs: between the mid-1970s and early 1990s, Colombia's harvest rose by 54 per cent, Costa Rica's 89 per cent and Honduras's by 140 per cent.[22] Rather than destroy excess coffee production, exporters disposed of it cheaply into markets not covered by the ICA, such as the Soviet Bloc. In 1989, 40 per cent of Costa Rica's crop was sold at half price or less and some was used as barter payment for goods such as Czechoslovakian buses.

Roasters' desire to access new supplies often resulted in a 'tourist' coffee arriving into a quota country via a non-quota one. Some further sleight of hand at the receiving port could result in high-grade coffee designated for a non-member country being swapped with low-grade coffee intended for a member one, so all parties obtained coffee at below-quota prices. The phenomena persisted because members were reluctant to adjust quotas at their own expense to reflect shifting demand.

In September 1989, with Soviet and Sandinista regimes fading, the United States withdrew its support for the quota system, eventually withdrawing from the ICO in 1993. It was the only consumer member to do so, but without it there was no way to implement a regulatory system. Meanwhile the contrasting interests of producer nations left few with any appetite to continue. Some state agencies were disbanded, notably the Brazilian IBC. Today, the ICO continues operating as an international information exchange, but lacks any global coffee supply chain governance role.

For all its dysfunctionality, the quota regime delivered relative stability. The monthly indicator price varied by 14.8 per cent during the last eight years of quotas; over the following eight years, variability was 37 per cent. Between 1984 and 1988 the average indicator price was $1.34/lb; between 1989 and 1993, as supplies flooded the market, that fell to $0.77.[23] Brazilian frosts halted the fall as supplies fell, but it was clear that the systemic instability of the global coffee trade had returned.

Vietnam

Vietnam exploited the ICA's demise, fundamentally changing the world coffee trade in the twentieth century's last decade. It became the world's second-largest coffee producer in 1999, overtaking Colombia, having ranked only 22nd in 1988. The key to its success was growing Robusta, of which the country became the world's largest exporter.

Missionaries planted small amounts of Arabica in the 1850s, but coffee remained a minor crop during French colonial rule. By 1975, at the end of the long war between the communist North and American-backed South, only 60 hectares (148 acres) of coffee remained. Following its victory, the Communist regime sought to stabilize areas formerly under southern control. Loyal North Vietnamese peasants were encouraged to

Vietnam, 1994. Farmers near Buon Ma Thuot in Vietnam's central highlands weighing dried Robusta coffee cherries.

migrate into the Central Highlands region where state farms and agricultural cooperatives were established, through a combination of nationalization of existing holdings and an aggressive deforestation programme. Here they were encouraged to grow coffee for export to Vietnam's Soviet Bloc allies.

It was only after the government economic reforms started in the 1980s that output began to soar. Transferring land into private hands during the 1990s meant that by 2000, 90 per cent of coffee production was undertaken by smallholders farming plots of less than 1 hectare (2½ acres). They were still strongly supported by the state, which continued to incentivize production through land subsidies, financial credits and technical assistance, such as access to fertilizers. This resulted in a remarkable average 24 per cent per annum growth in output between 1988 and 1999, and much higher average yields than competitor countries.

In 1995, Vinacafe, the state body responsible for the coffee industry, including development, marketing and export activity, was transformed into the Vietnamese National Coffee Corporation. It operates the remaining state farms as well as many processing, trading and service providers. It controls around 40 per cent of the country's exports, and operates one of the country's two instant coffee facilities (the other belongs to Nestlé).

The rapid expansion of Vietnamese production seemed designed to shore up the regime's political position in the wake of the Soviet Bloc's demise. It increased its export revenues while allowing peasants to 'enrich themselves' through direct market contact. The danger was that eventually the glut of supplies would drive down prices – as happened dramatically after 1998.

The Coffee Crisis

In 1998 the ICO's composite indicator price for coffee was 109 U.S. cents per pound; by 2002 it had fallen to below 48 cents. Although the price rose thereafter, it was only in 2007 that it returned above $1 to 107 cents. This dramatic and prolonged price collapse had profound effects. Producers were plunged into poverty, while the industry's public image in consumer countries came under attack.

The problem was an ongoing excess of supply over demand. In 2001–2, 113 million bags of coffee were produced, an additional 40 million bags had accumulated, yet world consumption stood at 106 million bags. The ICO executive director declared, 'At the origin of this coffee glut lies the rapid expansion of production in Vietnam and new plantations in Brazil.'[24]

The price fall consequences were felt differently across the sector. Where costs of production were low, technologies well developed and exchange rate movements favourable, such as in Brazil, it was still possible to make profits. Conversely, where coffee was used as a cash crop by subsistence farmers, as in most African, some Central American and many Asian countries, this reduced the money available to spend on medicines, education, food or servicing debts.

In Guatemala, the coffee labour force was halved. In Colombia, farmers ripped up their coffee trees, replacing them with coca plants for the drugs trade. Many Mexican growers gave up and attempted to illegally enter the U.S., often perishing in the attempt. Political conflicts intensified, with peasants in Chiapas, the centre of Mexican coffee production, supporting the Zapatista guerrilla movement's rebellion against the government.

Even in Vietnam, some farmers were forced to sell possessions to satisfy debt collectors. Poverty levels in the Central Highlands reached 50 per cent, with 30 per cent of the population suffering from hunger and malnutrition. Robusta's price fell from 83 cents in 1998 to just 28 cents in 2001. This had huge repercussions for countries like Uganda that were heavily dependent on exporting coffee.

Vietnamese output continued to expand, however, as peasants sought to produce their way out of the crisis. In 1990–91 the country produced 1.3 million bags, in 2000–2001 14.8 million bags, and by 2015–16 an astounding 28.7 million bags, more than the entire continent of Africa. Other Asian countries followed Vietnam's lead. The Southeast Asian countries Myanmar, Laos and Thailand developed significant coffee industries. Indonesia and India joined the ranks of the top six producers. In all these cases, over 90 per cent of the output is Robusta.

Coffee prices accelerated after 2010, when a virulent attack of coffee rust started spreading throughout Latin America. This has forced a rebalancing of supply and demand, particularly for high-quality Arabica, resulting in coffee's composite price remaining at over 120 cents per pound throughout the decade. It should not be forgotten that some of this new-found stability is at the expense of those forced out of farming, whether by falling prices, drought or disease.

Coffee's price volatility following the collapse of the quota system in 1989 is proof to many of the dangers of deregulation. Even the rust epidemic has been blamed on the demise of para-state agencies that coordinated national research and responses to crop disease.[25] Yet though the quota regime regulated coffee's flow onto the market, it favoured established producers, while state agencies frequently failed to pass back profits made from coffee to farmers.

The paradox that the so-called 'latte revolution', characterized by the rapid growth of coffee shops charging premium prices, coincided with the coffee crisis, provoked criticism of consuming 'poverty in your coffee cup'.[26] Others, though, saw this new phenomenon as an opportunity to recast coffee as a 'specialty beverage', facilitating its de-commodification, and the generation of greater revenues throughout the value chain.

6
A Specialty Beverage

The repositioning of coffee as a specialty beverage at the end of the twentieth century has had profound effects upon the global coffee industry. What began as a protest by independent roasters in the U.S. against commodification and industry concentration spawned the spread of international coffee shop chains, the hipster 'third wave' movement, the development of the coffee capsule, and a set of fierce debates about ethical coffee consumption. Arguably, the role of specialty in stimulating consumption in non-traditional markets has laid the foundations for a new era in coffee history.

The Birth of Specialty

In the United States, the four leading roasters' market share rose from 46 per cent in 1958 to 69 per cent in 1978. By 2000, the 'big three' – Procter & Gamble, Kraft, and Sara Lee – controlled over 80 per cent of the retail market. They competed on price: blend contents were cheapened, and some brands advertised that lower quantities of their product could be used to deliver the same brew strength.

These tactics failed to reverse the steady decline in U.S. coffee consumption per capita, which dropped from around 7.25 kilograms (16 lb) in 1960 to 2.7 kilograms (6 lb) by 1995, despite the success of the automatic Mr Coffee machine at converting Americans (especially men) to drip brewing in the 1970s. By contrast, consumption of caffeinated soft drinks boomed, for reasons as diverse as the spread of central heating, the rise of fast food outlets and the appeal of youthful advertising.

Independent roasters saw their numbers fall from around 1,500 in 1945 to 162 in 1972. To survive they evolved an alternative business strategy. Rather than price, they would compete on quality, enabling them to increase profit margins on their beans. Their approach suited a consumer economy in which different social groups had started using their purchases to convey messages about their lifestyles, values and tastes. These might include demonstrating sophistication or wealth; adherence to 'alternative', anti-corporate values; or a preference for 'authentic' artisan goods.

An early specialty coffee store in Seattle, 1977, selling beans for home consumption with no espresso machine in sight. Its name . . . Starbucks.

Coffee was an important ingredient of 1960s American counterculture, whose spiritual home lay in San Francisco. Hippies hung out at North Beach espresso bars run by Italian immigrants, and purchased their beans from Alfred Peet's store in Berkeley. Peet, a Dutchman, roasted his coffee considerably darker, and brewed it much stronger, than a regular 'cup of Joe'. Despite the proprietor's barely disguised disdain for many of his customers, Peet's became a mecca for those keen to experience 'European' coffee.

The first person to use the term 'specialty coffee' was Erna Knutsen. In the mid-1970s she convinced the San Francisco coffee importers where she had started as a secretary to allow her to try selling small lots of quality coffees. She found a niche supplying a new generation of independent roasters, many of whom had 'dropped out' from conventional career paths.

In 1982 a group of roasters founded the Specialty Coffee Association of America (SCAA), defining 'specialty' as delivering a distinctive taste in the cup. Their product ranges included high-grade export coffees such as Kenyan AA, alongside blends and flavoured coffees with names such as 'Swiss Mocha Almond' – all unlikely to be classed as specialty today. These were sold in gourmet delicatessens popular with 'yuppies' – the young urban professionals whose rising purchasing power underpinned the 1980s foodie revolutions.

Specialty coffee took off once emphasis switched from selling beans to serving beverages. Seattle was at the centre: in 1980 the first coffee carts incorporating espresso machines appeared in the city; by 1990 there were over two hundred carts positioned close to monorail stations, ferry terminals and major stores. Workers, it turned out, preferred to pay for takeaway specialty-style beverages than consume the free coffee available in their offices. Today only one or two carts remain, the others swept away by the coffee shop revolution that the city spread to the world.

The Origins of Starbucks

Starbucks was set up by three college friends in 1971. It primarily sold beans supplied by Alfred Peet, whose dark roasting style they subsequently adopted. Howard Schultz, a salesman for a Brooklyn company which was one of their equipment suppliers, visited in 1982 and convinced the founders to hire him as sales and marketing director. In 1983 Schultz visited Milan, where he

> found the inspiration and vision that have driven my own life, and the course of Starbucks . . . If we could re-create in America the authentic Italian coffee bar culture . . . Starbucks could be a great *experience*, and not just a great retail store.[1]

He failed to convince the Starbucks owners of his case, however, and left to open a coffee shop called *Il Giornale* in 1986. He chose the name believing it meant 'daily', in reference to the frequency with which Italians visit their local bar. In fact, it means 'newspaper'.

This was not the only element of Schultz's vision that did not translate. Customers did not want to stand sipping coffee at the counter, but to sit at a table and chat. They preferred paper cups to porcelain ones, so they could take their drinks back to work. Opera in the background and bow-tie-wearing baristas did not fit with the informal Pacific Northwest vibe.

Once Schultz adjusted his offer to create an 'Italian-style' experience that met American customer needs, he started to have success. In 1987 he transferred this format into Starbucks, which he bought when the last of the original founders left for San Francisco to take over Peet's.

Coffee Shop Format

The coffee shop format combines two elements: the coffee and the environment. The former pays for the latter.

Italian-style coffees proved perfect for introducing American consumers to specialty coffee, as the distinctive bite of the espresso could still be discerned through the sweetness of the milk. Caffè latte was the most popular, as steamed, rather than frothed, milk produces greater density and sweetness than in a cappuccino. The addition of flavoured syrups allowed shops to develop bespoke ranges and offer seasonal beverages such as eggnog latte. Approachability proved more important than authenticity: a Starbucks standard tall cappuccino is twice the size of an Italian one – further augmenting the sweetness.

By 1994 espresso-based beverages were outselling brewed coffees in U.S. specialty stores. The theatre of the barista 'hand-crafting' the beverage – grinding fresh beans, pulling a shot from the machine, foaming and pouring the milk, topping with cinnamon, chocolate and/or sprinkles – all rendered visible the value added during the process. Consequently, consumers were prepared to pay a high price for a premium product they could not make at home.

The high margins incorporated in the price paid for a comfortable environment in which the coffee could be enjoyed. Sofas, music, newspapers and clean toilets with baby-changing facilities all helped create a 'twenty-minute business'. Coffee is the rental charge for using the facilities provided by the shop. It feels democratic, as customers are served in order of arrival at the counter; and inclusive, as the focus on coffee rather than alcohol renders it a 'safe' space for women, children and non-drinkers.

Schultz trumpeted Starbucks as an exemplar of a 'third place' between work and home in which – as the sociologist Ray Oldenburg describes it – informal contacts between unrelated people create a sense of community.[2] Behavioural studies, however, find little evidence of conversations being initiated between strangers: the attraction of the coffee shop lies in being surrounded by people without having to engage with them. The continuing advances of digital technologies – the laptop computer, the mobile phone, the wireless Internet connection – allow individuals to continue working, or engage in social media conversation, while 'consuming' the coffee shop ambience.

The Hegemonic Chain

Schultz proved adept at raising capital for expansion. After an initial public offering of stock in the company in 1992, Starbucks concentrated on acquiring high footfall locations, frequently close to each other on the same street. This had the effect of growing overall trade, because people would not deviate far from their daily routines to get a coffee. Once converted to specialty coffee, however, they were disposed to drink it wherever they found it, boosting not just Starbucks' trade, but that of the whole sector.

Branding was critical to maintaining Starbucks' premium position. Guaranteeing customers the same experience whichever outlet they visited required staff to follow a customer service script and brew the same beverages consistently, hence Swiss super-automatic push-button espresso machines

Specialty Coffee Shops and Starbucks outlets in the USA[3]

Year	Specialty Coffee Shops	Starbucks Outlets	Proportion (%)
1989	585	46	7.9
1994	3,600	425	11.8
2000	12,600	2,776	22.0
2013	29,308	11,962	40.8

replaced the traditional Italian equipment in 1999. Celebrities were paid to be 'found' and photographed sipping coffee from branded takeaway cups. Starbucks maintained itself as the hegemonic brand within the coffee shop sector, and was so dominant that it effectively defined what consumers understood the coffee shop concept to mean.

In 2016, as many Americans reported drinking a 'gourmet coffee' or specialty coffee as a regular one the previous day.[4] This was driven by a threefold rise in the consumption of espresso-based beverages since 2008, which in turn reflected their adoption by everyday fast food chains and corner shops

Starbucks Reserve Roastery, Seattle, 2017. Featuring on-site roasting, augmented reality experiences and a huge range of beans and brewing methods, Reserve Roasteries are intended to promote the brand's credentials within the 'third wave' coffee culture.

such as Dunkin' Donuts and McDonald's. Caffè latte is now as much the American coffee style as a 'cup of Joe'.

Internationalization

Internationalization was the other key strand to the Starbucks strategy – on 1 January 2017 there were 25,734 stores operating in 75 countries. The first opened in Japan and Singapore in 1996, and the programme was quickly extended into other Southeast Asian 'tiger economies'. Coffee shop culture was warmly embraced by younger members of the middle classes, keen to emulate American trends by adopting them as hang-outs for socializing and studying.

In Europe, the coffee shop concept often travelled in advance of Starbucks, as imitators and émigrés adapted it to meet local tastes. Costa Coffee, a London-based coffee roaster supplying the Anglo-Italian café trade, started opening espresso bars in the late 1980s. In 1995 it was purchased by the brewing and leisure conglomerate Whitbread, which correctly foresaw that coffee shops would replace pubs as social hubs in Britain. From 41 outlets in 1995 Costa reached 2,100 in 2017, making it the largest operator. Like all chains in the UK, it employs largely foreign baristas: young people taking advantage of then current European Union laws on freedom of movement.[5]

Branded chains drove UK coffee shop growth, but since the 2010s the fastest-developing sector has been among department store and garden centre chains, reflecting the extent to which Italian-style coffee has become a mainstream British beverage. Pubs, whose numbers continue to decline, are now serving coffee during the day as a survival strategy.

Coffee shop chains have spread throughout the Continent, but their progress has been contingent on the character of local coffee cultures. In Germany, Vanessa Kullmann set up the first chain, Balzac Coffee, in 1998, after experiencing coffee shops as a fashion buyer in New York. Premium espresso beverages now constitute around 50 per cent of the German out-of-home market, but the majority are served in bakery chains. In France, where espresso-style beverages were well established, chains appeared in the 1990s, yet only really started to gain momentum as quick-service alternatives to bistros following the economic slump of 2008. The same occurred in Greece.

Italy, as the originator of espresso, has been a major beneficiary of the specialty revolution. Exports of roasted coffee rose from 12 million kg in 1988 to over 171 million kilograms in 2015. Italian companies control 70 per cent of the global market for commercial espresso machines, routinely exporting over 90 per cent of their output. Groups such as Illy and Segafredo have established branded chains throughout the

The Espresso martini: Dick Bradshaw, a London barman in the 1980s, came up with this cocktail when asked by a female customer for something that will 'wake me up, then f*** me up'.

An Italian-built espresso machine delivering coffee. The Italian Espresso National Institute (INEI) certifies baristas, blends and espresso equipment as capable of producing coffee to its legally registered standards, as indicated by its logo on the machine.

world using licensing and franchising options. In Italy itself, however, no coffee shop chains have emerged, as it would be impossible to charge a premium price for espresso. Starbucks is due to open in Milan in 2018, some 35 years after Schultz's revelatory visit, but using a format designed to highlight its 'third wave' credentials.

The Third Wave

The term 'third wave coffee' was first used by Timothy Castle in 2000, and popularized by Trish Rothgeb, an American roaster, in an influential article in 2003.[6] The first wave of mass-market roasters, she wrote, had 'made bad coffee commonplace'. The original specialty operators 'started destination shops with small roasting operations . . . serving espresso', but their format was eclipsed by second wave giants such as Starbucks who 'want to automate or homogenize specialty coffee'. The third wave would pursue a 'no rules' approach to crafting outstanding coffee.

Barista competitions are at the centre of third wave culture. The first World Barista Championships were held in Monaco in 2000. Competitors prepare a set of four espressos, cappuccinos and 'signature drinks' within fifteen minutes and are judged on technical and presentational skills, as well as the sensory qualities of their beverages. Equipment makers vie to have their machines classified as meeting competition standards. Roasters train baristas full time to compete using specially sourced blends. Winners gain celebrity status that bring high-paying contracts for consultancy and endorsements.

Third wave baristas experiment with the established parameters for espresso preparation and taste profiles, breaking away from Italian traditions. New beverages appeared as a result of those experimentations, such as the flat white, made

Seoul, South Korea. The 2017 World Barista Champion Dale Harris, from the United Kingdom, on the way to winning his title.

using concentrated shots of espresso topped with velvety microfoamed milk and finished with latte art – all demanding high technical skills from the barista. The flat white was brought to London in 2007 by baristas from Australia and by 2010 had crossed into the mainstream chains, later crossing the Atlantic.

Third wave coffee shops often operate on a shoestring, their owners inspired more by passion than profitability. Stripped-back interiors and basic seating highlight the high-tech machinery on the counter into which all the investment has been poured. This aggressively non-corporate ambience recurs so often that it has become the third wave's own brand image.

Third wave roasters source single-origin coffees from the same geographical district, preferably traceable back to a single farm or a producer cooperative. They take an artisan approach – roasting in small batches and adjusting profiles to achieve

The flat white evolved in Australia in the 1980s and was probably named to distinguish the flat velvety top from the dome of froth on top of a cappuccino. When cafés found it difficult to froth fresh milk, they put signs reading 'flat whites only'.

the best results from each lot. The roasts are usually light – designed to bring out the taste profiles of the beans, rather than draw attention to the roast's character itself.

In 1999 leading U.S. specialty buyers began organizing Cup of Excellence competitions in producer countries. Farmers submit their coffees to be assessed by an international jury of cuppers, with lots from the winners being auctioned online for astronomical prices. It is indicative of the global spread of specialty coffee that purchasers of the winning lots in the 2016 auctions came from Japan, Korea, Taiwan, Bulgaria, Australia, the Netherlands and the USA.

The third wave has increasingly shifted attention away from espresso to other forms of coffee brewing best able to bring out the subtleties of single-origin specialty grades. Equipment developed in Japan – such as the Hario V60 filter and the syphon brewer – has become common in third wave coffee shops. The Chemex, first manufactured during the 1940s, has acquired popularity, as its enhanced paper filters produce an exceptionally clean coffee resulting in beverages that can seem closer to tea.

The third wave can best be described as a form of transnational 'subculture', with its own mix of philosophies, iconic brands, fanzine-style publications and key influencers. The Internet has made this possible, enabling micro-roasters to find customers around the country – so-called 'prosumers' – to discuss the best ways to customize their machinery, and connoisseurs to read the latest coffee reviews online. These communities come together at coffee festivals such as that held in London since 2011.

Single-portion Coffee

The specialty revolution created a desire to prepare similar beverages in the home. Machines using 'single portion' coffee capsules have delivered this. Portions of ground coffee are sealed into aluminium capsules to preserve freshness. When placed into operating machines, the top of the capsule is punctured by pins and hot water is injected into it, causing the capsule to rupture under pressure as the coffee is delivered. Such systems combine convenience with cleanliness, but the capsules can only be recycled using specialized equipment, requiring consumers to make the commitment to collect and return them, rather than placing them in their household waste.

Nespresso, established by Nestlé in 1986, pioneered this technique for delivering espresso-style beverages, and remains the sector's global leader. In the U.S. market, the Keurig K-Cup system, introduced by Green Mountain Coffee Roasters in 1998, dominates the market for replicating American-style drip-brewed coffees.

Nespresso was developed for hospitality operators such as small restaurants, airlines and train companies, meeting their need for machines that did not require trained baristas or large amounts of space. Keurig was targeted to the office and hotel bedroom market, as providing pods prevented mess and waste. It soon became apparent, however, that these same advantages made the systems attractive to home users.

Nespresso positions its products as offering an entrée into the gourmet coffee world. Alongside espresso blends to suit a variety of palates and preferences, it offered so-called *grand cru* and limited-edition coffees to customers enrolled in its members' club. In 2000 the company opened its first retail boutique in Paris; by the end of 2015 there were 467 in sixty countries, occupying prime locations in major cities

An area of the Nespresso boutique in St Petersburg, Russia, with machines and capsules on display, 2017.

chosen for their proximity to luxury brand outlets. Co-branding strategies, such as the introduction of machines designed by Porsche, has cemented Nespresso as an upmarket lifestyle product, endorsed by George Clooney, who has been the principal brand ambassador since 2005.

Between 2000 and 2010 Nespresso experienced annual growth rates of over 30 per cent per annum. The premium it commands for its products is such that in 2010 Switzerland became the world's largest exporter of roasted coffee by value, even though it lies only fifth by volume.

In 2012 the patents protecting Nespresso and Keurig's proprietary technologies expired. In the five years thereafter, the global market for single-portion coffee grew by at least 50 per cent. Coffee shop chains capitalized on their brands by launching home systems, and manufacturers attempted to undercut Nespresso and Keurig by producing compatible pods, while artisan operators explored the potential of pods for third wave coffee. By 2017 at least a third of coffee-drinking households in the U.S. and UK were making use of capsule machines.

Ethical Coffee

Specialty coffee played the leading role in the adoption of certification systems whose labels attest to the environmental or socioeconomic sustainability of the supply chain for a particular coffee. Environmental certifications include Organic, Bird Friendly and Rainforest Alliance, which promote sustainable farming techniques that encourage biodiversity.

The first social certification programme was developed by the Fairtrade movement. In 1988 Solidaridad, a Dutch religious organization, established the Max Havelaar label – named after the novel denouncing the colonial coffee trade in Java. It started purchasing from producer cooperatives, initially in Mexico, and marketing the coffee in Germany and the Netherlands. In 1989 UK charities including Oxfam followed suit, creating the Cafédirect brand, and selling it through church halls and charity shops. In 1997 Fairtrade International was established to unite the various national schemes.

Fairtrade remains the only certification system to guarantee producers a minimum price for their coffee. Its pricing structures reflect whether the coffee is Arabica or Robusta, natural or washed, organic or non-organic. In addition, the exporting cooperative receives a social premium to be invested in improving the living conditions of the coffee-farming community. Since 2011 a quarter of this premium must be invested in improving quality. Should the world market price exceed the Fairtrade price at the time of delivery, then the higher price applies.

The Fairtrade organizations do not themselves buy or sell coffee. Instead they grant permission and charge for products to be labelled as 'Fairtrade'. For this to happen, all the participants in the commodity chain must be certified to ensure adherence to Fairtrade standards. Critics of Fairtrade argue

Fairtrade, organic coffee on sale in Slovenia's first Fairtrade shop, Ljubljana, 2013. The coffee is supplied by EZA, an Austrian social enterprise founded by Catholic social associations.

that the price guarantee induces inertia among producers by protecting them from the market and the need to respond to it. Furthermore, the bulk of the price differential paid by the consumer remains within the developed world, either with the roaster or supporting the operational costs of the certification systems.

Analysing the impact of Fairtrade certification systems upon producers has revealed mixed results. The floor price provided a significant safety net during the mid-2000s coffee crisis and many communities benefitted from the reinvestment of the social premium. Since then the gap between the Fairtrade and market price for coffee has remained relatively narrow. Research in Latin America suggests that this differential is not always sufficient to offset the potential losses in farmers' incomes from requirements to pay pickers better wages, and the organic premium does not make up for the reduced yields resulting from conversion.[7] A 2017 study discovered that while Fairtrade producers in Asia earn sufficient income to support their households, those in Africa cannot because their holdings are too small to reap the benefits of the premium.[8]

The value of the Fairtrade label to roasters and operators is that it demonstrates their ethical convictions, while enabling them to charge a premium that covers the additional purchase costs. They became particularly sensitive to this during the coffee crisis years, when the paradox of premium-priced lattes and starving coffee farmers was regularly highlighted in the media. This contributed to Starbucks being targeted during the antiglobalization riots in Seattle in 1999, although it was high-volume commodity roasters who were paying the least to their suppliers.

There was, however, relatively little Fairtrade coffee available, because of the organization's insistence that this should be sourced through producer cooperatives. This excluded a priori coffee from large plantations, independent farmers and smallholders who were not attached to cooperatives, as well as a significant number of cooperatives which were also put off by the initial certification costs.

Alternative certification schemes evolved that could be accessed by these producers, but left traders and producers to determine the premium placed upon the label. The Common Code for the Coffee Community (known as 4Cs), developed by large roasters and producer states, introduced a baseline set of social, environmental and economic standards in 2007. The price of 4C producer certification is graduated according to output, making it within the reach of many smallholders, while its easily achievable standards make it attractive to multinational corporations sourcing from multiple suppliers.

In 2012 Fairtrade USA broke away from Fairtrade International to enable it to certify non-cooperatively organized producers. It argued that this extended protection to labourers and independent smallholders, while offering more consumers the choice to buy Fairtrade.

By 2013 around 40 per cent of coffee's global production was in accordance with some form of certification standard.[9] Enthusiasts have argued that this represents one of the greatest triumphs of imposing social responsibility on global capitalism. Critics say this is a triumph of public relations, enabling the coffee industry to simultaneously monetize consumers' ethical concerns while engaging in 'virtue signalling'.

Third wave roasters object to Fairtrade's lack of concern with quality and traceability. Buyers for Stumptown, Intelligentsia and Counter Culture, leading third wave coffee roasters in the USA, developed an alternative model of 'direct trade': identifying growers of potentially outstanding coffee, working with them to ensure quality and purchasing from them directly at prices that reflect this, way beyond those achievable under Fairtrade. Such partnerships can be transformative in their impact on growers, but are confined to farmers in locations where cultivating specialty coffee is possible.

Interventions linking Fairtrade, direct trade and other development programmes have done much to improve conditions in certain countries. Rwanda's coffee infrastructure, which centred on commodity production, was destroyed during the 1994 genocide. In 2002 a national coffee strategy was introduced, investing in the installation of washing stations, part-financed by foreign aid programmes. Roasters have developed direct relationships with farmers and processors, investing in training and constructing cupping labs to test for quality. Fairtrade organizations have certified cooperatives that operate the washing stations.

Rwanda nearly doubled the value of its coffee exports between 2006 and 2012 because of the much higher prices enjoyed by fully washed coffees. Much of this additional

A coffee cupper at work in Rwanda. In 2002 a National Coffee Strategy was introduced with the aim of transforming the country from a commodity producer to a specialty one. By 2014 over 42 per cent of the country's coffee output was fully washed.

revenue is returned to producers; and encounters between farmers of different ethnicities using the washing stations have contributed to lowering tensions.[10] Rwanda is now widely recognized as a specialty producer; in 2008, it became the first African country to host a Cup of Excellence competition.

Globalizing Consumption

The specialty movement's greatest impact upon the global structures of coffee may well be its role in encouraging consumption in emerging economies, especially in producer states. By repositioning coffee as an aspirational beverage, it has become popular among younger, Western-orientated consumers.

V. G. Siddhartha opened the first outlets of Café Coffee Day, the Indian coffee shop chain in Bangalore, in 1996, tailoring them to a very specific demographic:

> We designed the place as one where students and youngsters would hang out. The internet was just coming in. We thought this would appeal to the software crowd in Bangalore, who had some international exposure. We started an internet service and gave the coffee free. Or we said, you buy a coffee you get half an hour internet service free . . . Seventy per cent of India is below the age of 35 as are 80 per cent of our customers . . . They want the same experience that they see in the movies or television or get through the internet.[11]

In 2015 Café Coffee Day was operating over 1,500 outlets in India. A critical part of both its business plan and customer proposition is growing its own coffee, controlling the process from crop to cup.

China is the market with most potential in Asia, by its size and current state of underdevelopment. Between 2004 and 2013 consumption grew by 16 per cent per annum, yet still only reached 83 grams per capita – enough for five or six cups of coffee *a year*, in what remains an overwhelmingly tea-drinking culture.

In the much smaller out-of-home sector, however, coffee accounts for 44 per cent of all sales. China already hosts the largest number of Starbucks outlets outside the USA, even though their clientele is largely confined to the wealthy urban middle class. Chinese consumers are particularly attracted to using their mobile phones to order 'social gifts' of cups of coffee for each other.

A branch of the Indian chain Café Coffee Day, 2006.

Currently nearly all at-home consumption is Robusta-based instant products, with half of all imports coming from Vietnam. The projected development of the country has seen major coffee companies such as Nestlé and Starbucks working with the Chinese Arabica farmers in Yunnan province in anticipation of offering local products to this growing market.

Brazil is the outstanding example of a producer country that has developed a consumer market. Some 95 per cent of adults consume coffee, and the country is close to overtaking the United States as the largest national market. All coffee sold in Brazil must have been grown in the country.

Annual average consumption rates have doubled between the 1990s and the 2010s. A driver for this is the rise of a new middle class that makes up nearly half the population. They have embraced the arrival of the new-style coffee shops serving cappuccinos, with out-of-home consumption rising by 170 per cent between 2003 and 2009. The introduction of independently certified quality labels for roast and ground coffees has transformed domestic consumption, raising both volume and quality.[12]

Roasters, retailers and coffee shop chains using local beans have sprung up in Indonesia, the Philippines and Vietnam, currently the fastest-growing consumer markets in Asia. Vietnam's Trung Nguyên Corporation operates five processing plants producing soluble products that it exports to over sixty countries. It owns or supplies over a thousand coffee shops in Vietnam. Most stores offer beverages brewed with Robusta-based powders and condensed milk, retaining their appeal to the local customer base.

The original tiger economies have moved on in their tastes. In Singapore, a well-established third wave culture reflects the city's global status. South Korea is currently the fastest-growing market for commercial espresso machines: Seoul supposedly has more coffee shops per capita than Seattle. Customers use them to escape their small apartments in the evenings, resulting in average visit lengths of over an hour, and opening times from 10 a.m. to 11 p.m.

A coffee nursery in Yunnan province, the heart of China's coffee-growing region, in 2014.

A New Era for Coffee?

The specialty movement developed as a countervailing tendency against coffee's commoditization in the developed world. Its success can be judged from the turnaround in U.S. per capita consumption, which returned to nearly 4.5 kilograms (10 lbs) in 2014.

Transnational corporations continue to dominate the industry, but there have been some significant shifts in their composition and character. Nestlé remains the largest roaster in the world, but its most dynamic element is Nespresso, which is positioned as a high-end specialty product. JAB, the Luxembourg-based private equity company whose portfolio of coffee brands includes JDE (Jacobs Douwe Egberts), has also invested in specialty, acquiring Peets and the 'third wave' chains Intelligentsia and Stumptown, as well as Keurig.

Coffee consumption is now much more evenly spread around the globe, breaking down the binary division between producer and consumer continents. Europe remains the largest continent with roughly a third of the market, but Asia, North America and Latin America each now command around a fifth. Given that per capita consumption rates in Asia are around one-tenth of those in North America, the potential for further development can be appreciated.

The impact of the specialty revolution is laying the foundations for a new era of coffee. Between 2014 and 2016, the world's annual consumption of coffee exceeded the quantity of beans produced. In the medium to long term the likelihood is that this trend will continue as demand for coffee, fuelled by the growth of new markets, increases, while output falls because of economic and environmental factors.

Economic development not only spurs coffee consumption, but impacts production. Coffee growers around the

Regional Distribution of World Coffee Consumption, 2012–16[13]

Region	Proportion of World Total (%)	Compound Annual Growth Rate (%)
Europe	33.3	1.2
Asia and Oceania	20.9	4.5
North America	18.4	2.5
South America	16.6	0.4
Africa	7.0	0.9
Central America	3.5	0.7
World	*100*	*1.9*

world are getting older as their sons and daughters migrate into the cities in search of better opportunities. This may lead to a decline in output, but could also address the issue of smallholdings becoming unsustainable when they are divided up between family members.

The biggest threat to coffee growing is climate change. It is estimated that there will be a 50 per cent reduction in the global area suitable for coffee production by 2050.[14] In addition to exceeding temperature extremes, increased climate volatility can affect yields through changes in rainfall patterns, disease and pest populations. While climate change may lead to new regions emerging – coffee is already being cultivated in southern California – the impacts on the traditional growing areas and the farmers they support will be profound. Scientific programmes to breed more climate-resistant varieties that retain good flavour profiles may help to mitigate these effects, but many farmers will still need to relocate or switch into other crops.

Such changes in the fundamentals underpinning the coffee market could potentially strengthen prices, particularly to

Coffee trading on the Ethiopian Commodity Exchange (ECX), 2017. The ECX was instituted to give Ethiopia greater opportunity to realize the value inherent in its coffees, though there have been disputes over the structures of its regulatory mechanisms.

those producers able to access the specialty market. They have already changed the geopolitical structures of the industry. For consumers, however, the benefits of the specialty revolution are that they can enjoy a greater quality and variety of coffee than has ever before been available. Happy brewing!

Recipes

It is easy to be intimidated into thinking that preparing a great cup of coffee requires lots of high-tech equipment, knowledge and a well-stuffed wallet. Here are some tips to 'up your coffee game' at home without too much time or money.

Freshness is key. The biggest change you can make is to start buying whole beans and grinding them just before use. Ideally use an electric burr grinder that can be calibrated to grind equally sized particles. Even an inexpensive single-blade 'knife' grinder will make a huge difference.

Purchase small amounts of beans and use them before they go stale. Check the bag for the coffee's roasting date (not the 'best before' date) – it should be no more than three weeks old. Store at room temperature in a dry, dark place – *not* the fridge!

You can buy beans in a supermarket, but try a specialty supplier by doing a web search on 'artisan coffee [your town]', or sign up for an online subscription service. Purchase 'single origin beans' from an identified country, preferably a named region such as Ethiopian Yirgacheffe.

If possible, use digital scales to weigh the coffee and water. Coffee scoops normally hold around 10 g ground coffee. Water temperature should be between 90 and 95 °C; a simple tip is to boil a kettle, then wait thirty seconds before using the water.

Suggested coffee and water brewing ratios
(approximate – dependent on taste)

Brewing Method	Serves	Ground Coffee (g)	Water (ml)	Brew time (mins)
French press	1	20	300	4
V60	1	18	250	3.5
Chemex	2–3	30	500	4
AeroPress (short)	1	15	150	0.5
AeroPress (long)	1	18	250	3.5
Espresso (shot)	1	7–9	25	25 seconds

French Press or Cafetière

The easiest and most forgiving way of brewing coffee. Grind the coffee coarse (think breadcrumbs), put it in the pot, add the heated water, cover, leave for four minutes (use a timer), then press the plunger down. Pour yourself a cup of flavourful coffee – perfect for breakfast.

Filter (V60, Chemex)

For a clean-tasting afternoon coffee, try a filter brewer such as the V60 or Chemex. Dampen the filter, add medium-ground coffee (think salt), shake level, pour a small amount of heated water to wet the coffee and wait for it to swell up or 'bloom'. Then gently pour over the remaining water at intervals and allow to drip through. Aim for two and a half minutes for a V60, four minutes for the Chemex.

AeroPress

The AeroPress is a great, portable device. Wet filter paper, attach filter basket to tube, stand on a mug, add medium-fine ground coffee then heated water, stir for ten seconds, insert plunger, push water through the coffee at a steady rate. For a concentrated cup, close to Americano, use AeroPress's scoop (approx. 15 grams) and add water to level number two. For a body between French press and filter, insert plunger into top of empty tube, turn upside down, add coffee and water, stir, steep three minutes, place mug over the top, turn over, press through slowly. Remove filter basket and blast the spent puck of coffee grounds out with the plunger.

Moka (Stovetop Espresso)

The secret to the stovetop Moka pot is to fill the bottom chamber to just below the air valve, loosely pack fine-ground coffee into the basket and turn the heat *off* once air is heard spluttering through the coffee into the upper chamber.

Espresso

Don't expect to make good espresso without investing heavily in machine and grinder. The grind (think sand) is vital because it controls the flow of the coffee: pre-ground espresso blends work better in a Moka. The basic principle of milk foaming is to insert the steam wand tip just under the surface of the milk, develop a vortex and then 'stretch' the milk by slowly lowering the milk jug, keeping the wand tip just under the surface of the milk. Coffee geeks love playing with their machines – you may find it quicker to visit your local coffee shop.

The Coffee Shop Menu

The international coffee shop menu is dominated by espresso-based beverages, in combination with milk that is either steamed or frothed (foamed). Milk foam varies from the highly airy macro-foam used in a 'dry' cappuccino to the velvety micro-foam with tiny bubbles used in the flat white. Serving sizes vary from country to country and chain to chain.

Americano	Hot water topped with an espresso shot
Babyccino	Frothed milk without coffee prepared for children
Caffè Latte	Espresso shot topped with steamed milk and a small head of foamed milk. Syrups are added to create flavours such as gingerbread, pumpkin or vanilla
Cappuccino	Espresso shot topped with equal portions of steamed and foamed milk. The domed head can be dusted with cocoa or cinnamon
Cold Brew	Long summer drink obtained by infusing cold water and coffee grounds in refrigerated conditions for between 16 and 24 hours
Cold Drip	Long drink obtained by filtering cold water through coffee at a very slow rate – typically eight hours
Cortado	Spanish-style espresso shot (longer and weaker than Italian), topped with an equal amount of steamed milk
Espresso	Concentrated shot of coffee, 25–30 ml brewed under approx. 9 bars of pressure. Many coffee shops now use a double espresso shot as standard
Flat White	The third wave's favourite milky coffee drink originated in Australasia. Micro-foamed milk is poured into a coffee cup containing a double ristretto, and the 'flat' top is usually finished with latte art
Iced Coffee	Regular brewed coffee chilled and served with ice
Macchiato	Espresso topped with a dash of foamed milk
Mocha	There are multiple variations, but the base elements are espresso, chocolate and steamed milk. Often served with marshmallows or similar additions

Nitro Coffee	Nitrogen-infused cold-brew coffee resulting in a creamy taste
Piccolo	Espresso shot topped with an equal proportion of micro-foamed milk
Ristretto	Short, strong espresso, approx. 15 ml, common in southern Italy

Coffee has long been used as an ingredient in food and cocktails. Here are a few historical recipes that demonstrate its versatility. All measures and instructions are as in the original.

Coffee Cake

From Mrs Beeton's *Book of Household Management* (1861)

½ lb butter
½ lb brown sugar
¼ lb golden syrup
½ lb currants
1 lb sultanas
1½ lb flour
1 oz. baking powder
2 eggs
½ oz. mix of nutmeg, cloves and cinnamon
coffee
a little milk

Sieve the baking powder and spices with the flour into a bowl; add the sugar and butter, rub well together, make a well in the centre, pour in the syrup, add about ¼ pint of strong, cold, coffee, break in the eggs, and beat well together; then mix in the other ingredients with a strong wooden spoon using a little milk if not moist enough, mix in the fruit last, and then bake in a long square cake-pan nicely prepared. Bake from 1 to 2 hours. Sufficient for a cake about 1¾ lb.

Coffee Ice Cream

From A. Escoffier, *A Guide to Modern Cookery* (1907)

Ice-cream preparation

Work ⅔ lb. of sugar and 10 egg yolks in a saucepan until the mixture reaches the ribbon-stage. Dilute it, little by little, with one quart of boiling milk, and stir over a moderate fire until the preparation veneers the withdrawn spoon. Avoid boiling, as it might decompose the custard. Strain the whole into a basin and stir it from time to time until it is quite cold.

To freeze an ice preparation . . . surround it with broken ice, mixed with sodium chloride (sea-salt or freezing salt) and saltpetre. The action of these two salts upon the ice causes a considerable drop in the temperature which speedily congeals any contiguous liquid . . . The freezer [i.e. the receptacle], in which the freezing takes place . . . should be of pure tin . . . pour into it the preparation to be frozen and then either keep it in motion by rocking the utensil to and fro, by grasping the handle on the cover . . . or by turning the handle if the utensil is on a central axle . . . the rotary movement of the utensil causes the preparation to splash continually against the sides of the freezer, where it rapidly congeals, and the congealed portions are removed by means of a special spatula, as quickly as they form, until the whole becomes a smooth and homogeneous mass.

Coffee Flavouring

Add 2 oz. of freshly grilled and crushed coffee seeds to the boiled milk, and let them infuse for 20 minutes. Or, with an equivalent amount of ground coffee and ½ pint of water, prepare a very strong infusion and add it to 1½ pints of boiled milk.

Tiramisu

Tiramisu is considered a classic Italian dessert, but it was created in a Treviso restaurant in the 1970s. Here is the original restaurant recipe, available at www.tiramesu.it, which uses *savoiardi* biscuits (ladyfingers or sponge fingers).

12 egg yolks
500 g white sugar
1 kg mascarpone cheese
60 *savoiardi*
coffee
cocoa powder

Make coffee, set aside and let cool in a bowl. Whip egg yolks with sugar until stiff; fold mascarpone into the mixture to create a soft cream. Dip 30 *savoiardi* into the coffee, being careful not to soak them. Arrange them in a line, in the middle of a round dish. Spread half of the cream over the *savoiardi*. Repeat using remaining *savoiardi* and cream to create a second layer on top of the first. Sprinkle with cocoa powder and serve chilled.

Bruleau, aka Brûlot, aka Café Diabolique

From Martha McCulloch-Williams, *Dishes and Beverages of the Old South* (1913)

Put into the special bruleau bowl, which has its own brandy ladle, three ladlefuls of brandy, along with the yellow peel of half an orange, a dozen cloves, a stick of cinnamon, a few grains of allspice and six lumps of sugar. Let stand several hours to extract the essential oils. At serving time put in an extra ladleful of brandy for every person to be served, and two lumps of domino sugar. Pour alcohol in the tray underneath the bowl, light it, and stir the brandy back and forth until it also catches from the flame below. Let burn two or three minutes – if the lights be extinguished as they should be, the effect is beautifully spectral. After the three minutes pour in strong, hot, clear, black coffee, a small cupful for each person, keep stirring until the flame dies out, then serve literally blazing hot. This 'burnt water' known in more sophisticated regions as *Café Diabolique*, originated in New Orleans, and is the consummate flowering of Creole cookery.

Irish Coffee

When a transatlantic flying boat arrived into Foynes airport in Ireland in the 1940s, the airport barman added whiskey to his coffee to warm the passengers up. Asked if it was Brazilian coffee, he replied, 'No, Irish.' The recipe subsequently evolved in Ireland and the United States. Here is the version recommended by the Pan-American Coffee Bureau in its 1956 publication *Fun with Coffee*.

Into a warmed table wine glass, place 2 teaspoons of white sugar and fill glass about two-thirds with coffee. Mix. Add about 2 tablespoons of Irish whiskey and top with softly whipped cream. (To float the cream on top of the coffee, try pouring it over the back of a spoon – do not stir once in place.)

Espresso Martini

30 ml (1 shot) espresso
50 ml (2 fl. oz) vodka
10 ml (2 tsp) sugar syrup

Place all ingredients into a cocktail shaker filled with ice, and shake for at least 10 seconds. Pour into a chilled martini glass and garnish with three coffee beans placed close to each other.

References

Introduction

1 Data derived from Benoit Daviron and Stefano Ponte, *The Coffee Paradox* (London, 2005), p. 58; ICO data.

1 Seed to Cup

1 David Browning and Shirin Moayyad, 'Social Sustainability', in *The Craft and Science of Coffee*, ed. B. Folmer (Amsterdam, 2017), p. 109.

2 Nick Brown, 'Natural Geisha Breaks Best of Panama Auction Record at $803 per pound', www.dailycoffeenews.com, 20 July 2018.

3 Charles Lambot et al., 'Cultivating Coffee Quality', in *Craft and Science*, ed. Folmer, pp. 21–2.

4 Shawn Steiman, 'Why Does Coffee Taste That Way', in *Coffee: A Comprehensive Guide*, ed. R. Thurston, J. Morris and S. Steiman (Lanham, MD, 2013), p. 298.

5 'Applied R and D for Coffee Leaf Rust', www.worldcoffeeresearch.org, accessed 10 December 2004.

6 Oxfam, *Mugged: Poverty in Your Coffee Cup* (Oxford, 2002), p. 20.

7 Eric Nadelberg et al., 'Trading and Transaction', in *Craft and Science*, ed. Folmer, p. 207.

8 U.S. Department of Health and Human Services and U.S. Department of Agriculture, *2015–2020 Dietary Guidelines for Americans*, 8th edn (2015), p. 33, www.health.gov/dietaryguidelines/2015/guidelines.

8 Joseph Alpert, 'Hey Doc, is it OK for me to Drink Coffee?', *American Journal of Medicine*, CXXII/7 (2009), pp. 597–8.

2 Wine of Islam

1 Ralph Hattox, *Coffee and Coffeehouses: The Origins of a Social Beverage in the Medieval Near East* (Seattle, WA, 1985), p. 14.

2 Ibid., p. 18.

3 Ibid., p. 59.

4 Bernard Lewis, *Istanbul and the Civilization of the Ottoman Empire* (Norman, OK, 1963), p. 133.

5 Hattox, *Coffee and Coffeehouses*, p. 99.

6 Ayse Saracgil, 'Generi voluttari e ragion di stato', *Turcia*, 28 (1996), pp. 166–8.

7 Ibid., p. 167.

8 Ibid.

9 Ibid.

10 Michel Tuchscherer, 'Coffee in the Red Sea Area from the Sixteenth to the Nineteenth Century', in *The Global Coffee Economy in Africa, Asia, and Latin America, 1500–1989*, ed. William Gervase Clarence Smith and Steven Topik (Cambridge, 2003), p. 51.

11 Ibid., p. 55.

3 Colonial Good

1 Data derived from literature survey.

2 Markman Ellis, *The Coffee House: A Cultural History* (London, 2004), p. 82.

3 Bennet Alan Weinberg and Bonnie K. Bealer, *The World of Caffeine* (New York, 2002), pp. 74–9.

4 Karl Teply, *Die Einführung des Kaffees in Wien* (Vienna, 1980); Andreas Weigl, 'Vom Kaffehaus zum Beisl', in *Die Revolution am Esstisch*, ed. Hans Jürgen Teuteberg (Stuttgart, 2004), p. 180.

5 Ellis, *The Coffee House*, p. 33.

6 *The Vertue of the Coffee Drink* (London, undated, possibly 1656), now in the British Library.

7 Ellis, *The Coffee House*, p. 73.

8 Brian Cowan, *The Social Life of Coffee: The Emergence of the British Coffeehouse* (New Haven, CT, and London, 2005), p. 90.

9 *A Catalogue of the Rarities to Be Seen in Don Saltero's Coffee House in Chelsea* (London, 1731).

10 Samuel Pepys, diary entry, Friday 23 January 1663, www.pepysdiary.com.

11 Philippe Sylvestre Dufour, *Traitez nouveaux et curieux du café, du thé et du chocolat*, 3rd edn (The Hague, 1693), p. 135.

12 Julia Landweber, 'Domesticating the Queen of Beans', *World History Bulletin*, XXVI/1 (2010), p. 11.

13 Anne McCants, 'Poor Consumers as Global Consumers: The Diffusion of Tea and Coffee Drinking in the Eighteenth Century', *Economic History Review*, LXI, S1 (2008), p. 177.

14 M. R. Fernando, 'Coffee Cultivation in Java', in *The Global Coffee Economy in Africa, Asia and Latin America, 1500–1989*, ed. William Gervase Clarence Smith and Steven Topik (Cambridge, 2003), pp. 157–72.

15 Steven Topik, 'The Integration of the World Coffee Market', in *The Global Coffee Economy*, p. 28.

16 Gwyn Campbell, 'The Origins and Development of Coffee Production in Réunion and Madagascar', in *The Global Coffee Economy*, p. 68.

17 Emma Spary, *Eating the Enlightenment* (Chicago, IL, 2012), p. 91.

18 P. J. Laborie, *The Coffee Planter of Saint Domingo* (London, 1798), p. 158.

19 W. H. Ukers, *All About Coffee* (New York, 1935), p. 554.

20 Enrico Maltoni and Mauro Carli, *Coffeemakers* (Rimini, 2013).

21 Multatuli, *Max Havelaar: Or the Coffee Auctions of a Dutch Trading Company* [1860] (London, 1987).
22 Donovan Moldrich, *Bitter Berry Bondage: The Nineteenth Century Coffee Workers of Sri Lanka* (Pelawatta, Sri Lanka, 2016).

4 Industrial Product

1 Derived from William H. Ukers, *All About Coffee* (New York, 1935), p. 529; Mario Samper, 'Appendix: Historical Statistics of Coffee Production and Trade from 1700 to 1960', in *The Global Coffee Economy in Africa, Asia, and Latin America, 1500–1989*, ed. William Gervase Clarence Smith and Steven Topik (Cambridge, 2003), pp. 419, 442–4.
2 Steven Topik and Michelle McDonald, 'Why Americans Drink Coffee', in *Coffee: A Comprehensive Guide to the Bean, the Beverage and the Industry*, ed. R. Thurston, J. Morris and S. Steiman (Lanham, MD, 2013), p. 236.
3 Figures derived from William H. Ukers, *All About Coffee*, p. 529.
4 John D. Billings, *Hardtack and Coffee* (Boston, MA, 1887), pp. 129–30.
5 Jon Grinspan, 'How Coffee Fueled the Civil War', www.nytimes.com, 9 July 2014.
6 Ukers, *All About Coffee*, p. 589.
7 Ibid., p. 596.
8 Mark Prendergast, *Uncommon Grounds* (New York, 2010), p. 49.
9 Ibid., p. 71.
10 Data from Francisco Vidal Luna and Herbert S. Klein, *The Economic and Social History of Brazil since 1889* (Cambridge, 2014), pp. 355–9.
11 Francisco Vidal Luna, Herbert S. Klein and William Summerhill, 'The Characteristics of Coffee Production and Agriculture in the State of Sao Paolo in 1905', *Agricultural History*, XC/1 (2016), pp. 22–50.

12 Prendergast, *Uncommon Grounds*, p. 84.
13 William Roseberry, 'Introduction', in *Coffee, Society and Power in Latin America*, ed. W. Roseberry, L. Gudmondson and M. Samper Kutschbach (Baltimore, MD, 1995), p. 30.
14 Ukers, *All About Coffee*, p. 424.
15 Marco Palacios, *Coffee in Colombia, 1850–1970* (Cambridge, 1980), p. 217.
16 Paul C. Daniels, 'The Inter-American Coffee Agreement', *Law and Contemporary Problems*, 8 (1941), p. 720.
17 Prendergast, *Uncommon Grounds*, p. 157.
18 Ukers, *All About Coffee*, p. 484.
19 Prendergast, *Uncommon Grounds*, pp. 193–6.
20 Steve Lanford and Robert Mills, *Hills Bros. Coffee Can Chronology Field Guide* (Fairbanks, AK, 2006), pp. 19–25.
21 Andrés Uribe, *Brown Gold: The Amazing Story of Coffee* (New York, 1954), pp. 42–4.

5 Global Commodity

1 Data courtesy ICO, 1965/6 to 2016–17. Note 1960s = crop years 1965–6 to 1969–70; 2010s = crop years 2010/11 to 2016/17.
2 Stuart McCook, 'The Ecology of Taste', in *Coffee: A Comprehensive Guide*, ed. R. Thurston, J. Morris and S. Steiman (Lanham, MD, 2013), p. 253.
3 Jennifer A. Widner, 'The Origins of Agricultural Policy in Cote d'Ivoire', *Journal of Development Studies*, XXIX/4 (1993), pp. 25–59.
4 Moses Masiga and Alice Ruhweza, 'Commodity Revenue Management: Coffee and Cotton in Uganda', *International Institute for Sustainable Development* (2007).
5 Nestlé, *Over a Cup of Coffee* (Vevey, 2013), pp. 25–30.
6 Claire Beal, 'Should the Gold Blend Couple Get Back Together?', www.independent.co.uk, 28 April 2010.
7 Vivian Constantinopoulos and Daniel Young, *Frappé Nation* (Potamos, 2006).

8 Julia Rischbieter, '(Trans)National Consumer Cultures: Coffee as a Colonial Product in the German Kaiserreich', in *Hybrid Cultures – Nervous States*, ed. U. Lindner et al. (Amsterdam, 2010), pp. 109–10.

9 Dorothee Wierling, 'Coffee Worlds', *German Historical Institute London Bulletin*, XXXCI/2 (November 2014), pp. 24–48.

10 L. Whitaker, 'Coffee Drinking and Visiting Ceremonial Among the Karesuando Lapps', *Svenska landsmål och svenstkt folkiv* (1970), pp. 36–40.

11 Dannie Kjeldgaard and Jacob Ostberg, 'Coffee Grounds and the Global Cup: Global Consumer Culture in Scandinavia', *Consumption, Markets and Culture*, X/2 (2007), pp. 175–87.

12 Jonathan Morris, 'Making Italian Espresso, Making Espresso Italian', *Food and History*, VIII/2 (2010), pp. 155–83.

13 Charlotte Ashby, Tag Gronberg and Simon Shaw-Miller, eds, *The Viennese Café and Fin-de-siècle Culture* (London, 2013).

14 Harold B. Segel, *The Vienna Coffeehouse Wits, 1890–1938* (West Lafayette, IN, 1993), p. 11.

15 Merry White, *Coffee Life in Japan* (Berkeley, CA, 2012).

16 All Japan Coffee Association, 'Coffee Market in Japan', pdf document, www.coffee.ajca.or.jp/English, accessed 21 August 2017.

17 Gregory Dicum and Nina Luttinger, *The Coffee Book* (New York, 1999), p. 86.

18 Richard Bilder, 'The International Coffee Agreement', *Law and Contemporary Problems*, XXVIII/2 (1963), p. 378.

19 Steven Topik, John M. Talbot and Mario Samper, 'Globalization, Neoliberalism, and the Latin American Coffee Societies', *Latin American Perspectives*, XXXVII/2 (2010), p. 12.

20 Mark Prendergast, *Uncommon Grounds* (New York, 2010), p. 317.

21 John M. Talbot, *Grounds for Agreement* (Lanham, MD, 2004), p. 61.

22 Ibid., pp. 77–81.

23 International Coffee Organization, *World Coffee Trade (1963–2013): A Review of the Markets, Challenges and Opportunities Facing the Sector* (London, 2014).

24 Néstor Osorio, 'The Global Coffee Crisis: A Threat to Sustainable Development', Submission to World Summit on Sustainable Development (Johannesburg, 2002).

25 Stuart McCook and John Vandermeer, 'The Big Rust and the Red Queen', *Phytopathology Review*, CV (2015), pp. 1164–73.

26 Oxfam, *Mugged: Poverty in Your Coffee Cup* (Oxford, 2002).

6 A Specialty Beverage

1 Howard Schultz and Dori Jones Lang, *Pour Your Heart Into It* (New York, 1997), p. 52.

2 Ray Oldenburg, *The Great Good Place* (New York, 1989).

3 Data available at www.sca.org and www.statista.com.

4 'What Are We Drinking? Understanding Coffee Consumption Trends', www.nationalcoffeeblog.org, 2016.

5 Jonathan Morris, 'Why Espresso? Explaining Changes in European Coffee Preferences', *European Review of History*, XX/5 (2013), pp. 881–901.

6 Timothy J. Castle and Christopher M. Lee, 'The Coming Third Wave of Coffee Shops', *Tea and Coffee Asia* (December 1999–February 2000), p. 14; Trish Rothgeb Skeie, 'Norway and Coffee', *The Flamekeeper: Newsletter of the Roasters Guild*, SCAA (Spring 2003).

7 Daniel Jaffee, *Brewing Justice* (Berkeley, CA, 2007); Tina Beuchelt and Manfred Zeller, 'Profits and Poverty', *Ecological Economics*, LXX (2011), pp. 1316–24.

8 True Price, *Assessing Coffee Farmer Income* (Amsterdam, 2017).

9 David Levy et al., 'The Political Dynamics of Sustainable Coffee', *Journal of Management Studies*, LIII/3 (May 2016), p. 375.

10 Karol C. Boudreaux, 'A Better Brew for Success: Economic Liberalization in Rwanda's Coffee Sector', in *Yes Africa Can: Success Stories from a Dynamic Continent* (World Bank, 2010), pp. 185–99.

11 Ashis Mishra, 'Business Model for Indian Retail Sector', IIMB *Management Review*, xxv (2013), pp. 165–6.

12 International Coffee Organization, *A Step-by-step Guide to Promote Coffee Consumption in Producing Countries* (London, 2004), pp. 154–207; 'Brazil', www.thecoffeeguide.org, March 2011.

13 Data courtesy of ICO.

14 World Coffee Research, *The Future of Coffee: Annual Report 2016*, www.worldcoffeeresearch.org.

Select Bibliography

Clarence Smith, William Gervase, and Steven Topik, eds, *The Global Coffee Economy in Africa, Asia, and Latin America, 1500–1989* (Cambridge, 2003)

Daviron, Benoit, and Stefano Ponte, *The Coffee Paradox* (London, 2005)

Ellis, Markman, *The Coffee House: A Cultural History* (London, 2004)

Folmer, Britta, ed., *The Craft and Science of Coffee* (Amsterdam, 2017)

Hattox, Ralph, *Coffee and Coffeehouses: The Origins of a Social Beverage in the Medieval Near East* (Seattle, WA, 1985)

Laborie, P. J., *The Coffee Planter of Saint Domingo* (London, 1798)

Maltoni, Enrico, and Mauro Carli, *Coffeemakers* (Rimini, 2013)

Palalcios, Marco, *Coffee in Colombia 1850–1970* (Cambridge, 1980)

Prendergast, Mark, *Uncommon Grounds* (New York, 2010)

Roseberry, William, Lowell Gudmondson and Mario Samper Kutschbach, eds, *Coffee, Society and Power in Latin America* (Baltimore, MD, 1995)

Talbot, John M., *Grounds for Agreement* (Lanham, MD, 2004)

Thurston, Robert, Jonathan Morris and Shawn Steiman, eds, *Coffee: A Comprehensive Guide to the Bean, the Beverage and the Industry* (Lanham, MD, 2013)

Ukers, William H., *All About Coffee* (New York, 1935)

Vidal Luna, Francisco, and Herbert S. Klein, *The Economic and Social History of Brazil since 1889* (Cambridge, 2014)

Websites and Associations

Allegra World Coffee Portal
www.worldcoffeeportal.com

Comunicaffe International
www.comunicaffe.com

Global Coffee Report
www.gcrmag.com

International Coffee Organization
www.ico.org

National Coffee Association
www.ncausa.org

Perfect Daily Grind
www.perfectdailygrind.com

Specialty Coffee Association
www.sca.coffee

Tea and Coffee Trade Journal
www.teaandcoffee.net

World Coffee Research
www.worldcoffeeresearch.org

Acknowledgements

Writing this book has been like brewing an espresso: a huge amount of material has had to be concentrated down to produce an easily consumed final shot.

I'd like to thank Michael Leaman for commissioning this volume and giving me the time to prepare it properly, and the staff at Reaktion for all their assistance. Allegra Strategies, Comunicaffè, the International Coffee Organisation, the MUMAC Academy, the Specialty Coffee Association and World Coffee Research have all generously shared information with me, while I continue to be astounded by the generosity of the many members of the coffee industry from whom I've learned along the way. I am especially grateful to Ago Luggeri, Anna Hammerin, Anya Marco, Arthur Ernesto Darboven, Barbara Derboven, Barry Kither, Britta Folmer, Clive Maton, Colin Smith, Darcio De Camillis, Enzo Frangiamore, Ender Turan, Enrico Maltoni, Kenneth McAlpine, Kent Bakke, Lindsay Eynon, Luigi Morello, Maurizio Giuli, Robert Thurston, Shawn Steiman and Yasmin Silverman for their advice on specific aspects of this text.

This book would never have seen the light of day without the support of my wife, Elizabeth. I am blessed to share my coffee with her.

Photo Acknowledgements

The author and publishers wish to express their thanks to the below sources of illustrative material and/or permission to reproduce it. Some locations of artworks are also given below, in the interests of brevity:

Bettmann/Contributor/Getty Images: p. 119; © Château des ducs de Bretagne – Musée d'histoire de Nantes: p. 84; DeAgostini/ G. DAGLI ORTI/Contributor: p. 103; Elizabeth Dalziel: p. 41; Peter Harris/SteamPunkCoffeeMachine: p. 9; International Coffee Organization: pp. 19, 33, 109, 112, 123, 125, 131, 144; Keystone-France/ Gamma-Keystone via Getty Images: p. 107; Lebrecht Music and Arts Photo Library/Alamy Stock Photo: p. 76; Library of Congress, Washington, DC: pp. 44, 90; Stuart McCook: pp. 96, 99; Jonathan Morris: pp. 23, 26, 35, 37, 51, 137, 160, 162; © Nespresso: p. 165; courtesy Nestlé Historical Archives, Vevey, Switzerland: p. 127; Jake Olson for World Coffee Events: p. 161; © Paulig Coffee: p. 133; John Phillips/The LIFE Picture Collection/Getty Images: p. 105; Steve Raymer/CORBIS/Corbis via Getty Images: p. 147; Rijksmuseum, Amsterdam: pp. 56, 64, 79 (top and bottom); Kurt Severin/ Three Lions/Hulton Archive/Getty Images: p. 104; Colin Smith: pp. 14, 15 (top and bottom), 17, 21, 24 (top and bottom), 25, 27, 29, 30, 31, 46, 172, 176; © Specialty Coffee Association: pp. 10–11; Tatjana Splichal/Shutterstock.com: p. 167; Anthony Stewart/ National Geographic/Getty Images: p. 136; Robert Thurston: p. 173; Universal Images Group North America

LLC/DeAgostini/Alamy Stock Photo: p. 57; © Victoria and Albert Museum, London: p. 56; Victor Key Photos/Shutterstock: p. 159; World History Archive/Alamy Stock Photo: p. 81; Yale Center for British Art: p. 71.

Boston Public Library, the copyright holder of the image on p. 100; Rob Bertholf, the copyright holder of the image on p. 157; and Seattle Municipal Library, the copyright holder of the image on p. 152, have published them online under conditions imposed by a Creative Commons Attribution-Share Alike 2.0 Generic License; Howard F. Schwartz, Colorado State University, Bugwood.org, the copyright holder of the image on p. 88, has published it online under conditions imposed by a Creative Commons Attribution-Share Alike 3.0 Generic License; Andy Carlton, the copyright holder of the image on p. 170; Nesnad, the copyright holder of the image on p. 141; and Wellcome Images, the copyright holder of the image on p. 60, have published them online under conditions imposed by a Creative Commons Attribution-Share Alike 4.0 Generic License.

Readers are free:

> to share – to copy, distribute and transmit the work
> to remix – to adapt this image alone

Under the following conditions:

> attribution – You must attribute the work in the manner specified by the author or licensor (but not in any way that suggests that they endorse you or your use of the work).
>
> share alike – If you alter, transform, or build upon this work, you may distribute the resulting work only under the same or similar license to this one.

Index

italic numbers refer to illustrations; **bold** to recipes

MORE IN THE SERIES